Kids Outdoors

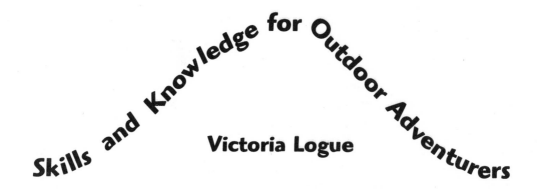

Skills and Knowledge for Outdoor Adventurers

Victoria Logue

Frank Logue

Mark Carroll

Ragged Mountain Press
Camden, Maine

To Tannika, Sara Ann, Margaret,

Nichole, Juliet, Kristin, Elisa, Bryan, Anthony,

Paul, Ben, Will, and the rest of the youth at St. Peter's Church in Rome, Georgia.

Thanks for keeping us young, if prematurely gray.

International Marine/
Ragged Mountain Press

A Division of The McGraw-Hill Companies

10 9 8 7 6 5 4 3 2

Library of Congress Cataloging-in-Publication Data
Logue, Victoria, 1961–
    Kids outdoors : the totally nonboring backcountry
skills guide / Victoria Logue, Frank Logue, Mark
Carroll.
        p.   cm.
    Includes index.
    Summary: Discusses the equipment and skills need-
ed to enjoy hiking and camping in wilderness areas.
Includes related activities and projects.
    ISBN 0-07-038477-0
    1. Backpacking—Juvenile literature. 2. Wilderness
survival–Juvenile literature. [1. Backpacking. 2.
Camping. 3. Outdoor recreation. 4. Wilderness survival.]   I. Logue, Frank, 1963–   . II. Carroll, Mark,
1950–   . III. Title.
GV199.6.L65   1996
796.5'2—dc20   96–33889
                                         CIP
                                         AC

Questions regarding the content of this book
should be addressed to:
    Ragged Mountain Press
    P.O. Box 220
    Camden, ME 04843

Questions regarding the ordering of this book
should be addressed to:
    The McGraw-Hill Companies
    Customer Service Department
    P.O. Box 547
    Blacklick, OH 43004
    Retail customers: 1-800-262-4729
    Bookstores: 1-800-233-4726

A portion of the profits from the sale of each Ragged
Mountain Press book is donated to an environmental
cause.

♻ Kids Outdoors is printed on 60-pound Renew
Opaque Vellum, an acid-free paper that contains
50 percent recycled waste paper (preconsumer) and
10 percent postconsumer waste paper.

Kids Outdoors is set in 10 point Adobe Bauer Bodoni

Printed by R.R. Donnelley, Crawfordsville, IN
Illustrations on pages 8, 14, 18, 31, 39, 58, 59, 79–83, 88,
        89, 90, 92, and 112 by Laurie Davis
Illustrations on pages 9, 13, 38, 40, 41, 44, 45, 50, 95–98,
        103, 120, and 121 by Melanie Pratt
All other illustrations by Mark Carroll
Design and Production by Dan Kirchoff
Edited by Jonathan Eaton, Jacqueline Boyle, Tom McCarthy

Contents

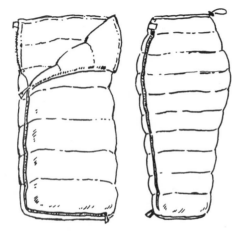

Kids
Outdoors

Introduction

Wooooooo! The plaintive call of a coyote cuts through the still night. It is a cry wilder than any description, not just heard, but felt. The sound reaches a place so deep inside you that it must be awakening some ancient DNA code. What you feel is not dread, or fear, but longing.

We don't hear the cry from the back porch of a hunting lodge or from a vehicle speeding down the interstate. A cool breeze is blowing and the late August moon is full, illuminating the Appalachian Trail on Maine's Gulf Hagas summit. A second coyote cries in the distance, followed by a chorus of them. It is impossible not to get caught up in the refrain, an unabashed celebration of the night's wildness. There are four of us on this moonlit hike, and we all return the coyotes' cries. Far from being scared away, the coyotes continue to howl and their cries even grow closer.

A few days later we're riding down I-95 when a coyote runs across the road, stops to look back at the highway, and dashes into the woods. He looks small and scared, and his presence there adds a note of sadness to the chorus we heard earlier in the week. We didn't hear the call of coyotes who know only the wild; they were less than a day's loping travel from a place where the wilderness had been tamed, "developed." Once wilderness is developed, it's gone.

Sharing the night with coyotes deep in roadless woods isn't for everyone. And a good thing it isn't! But you and I aren't content to travel within the confines of malls and other pavement-ringed palaces of a climate-controlled life. Hearing the coyote's wild cry, we're drawn toward it, not away. Backcountry travel takes resourcefulness—a self-reliance bred not from ignorance of the dangers, but from the knowledge needed to take care of ourselves. We know we'll get dirty, wet, and tired, but we know the rewards too.

Cold water tastes better from a high mountain spring than it ever can from a kitchen faucet. Stories from other camping trips told in the soft glow of a candle lantern have a power that shrivels under a school room's fluorescent lights. And the haunting sound of a coyote crying to the moon in the wilds of western Maine is unimaginable to people who see the moon only through the glare of city lights.

About This Book

This book is for leaders—people with the ability to make decisions quickly, who take action instead of following the crowd. It will give you the skills you need to lead adventures in the outdoors instead of just tagging along.

Throughout the book you will find ideas for activities that will help you have fun in the outdoors. Most of these projects are to be done at home and are not intended to try on a backcountry trip. For example, creating a plaster cast of animal tracks is a worthwhile exercise, but you won't want to pack the necessary supplies to some wilderness far from the nearest road. That's a project better suited to a nearby park. Others, like making fire starters, are things you can do at home to prepare for a camping trip. On the other hand, the tips about predicting the weather are most valuable when you're far from the nearest TV weather report.

Use this book to round out your abilities so you can lead the way into the backcountry for more adventures!

On the Trail

If you can walk, backpacking is simple—much easier to learn than cross-country skiing or in-line skating, which require new skills. But you have to consider your walking more carefully than usual when you're backpacking. For example, you don't have to worry about dehydration when you're walking around the mall, but on the trail it can be a real concern. Make sure you drink a little water at every break, even if you don't feel thirsty. By the time you start to feel thirsty, your body is already nearly a liter low on water, and that could lead to more serious conditions. Keeping yourself well hydrated will make the hiking easier too.

Take Breaks

When you first start hiking you will need frequent breaks, but soon you won't have to stop quite as often. One way to take a break, particularly during a tough uphill trail section, is with your pack on. Slowly lean over and hold your knees to take the weight off your hips and shoulders. The pack-on break will give you a little rest when you don't want to break your momentum by taking off your pack and sitting by the side of the trail. On steep sections, turn around and face downhill to rest tense muscles.

Stay on the Trail

Sometimes it's hard to tell the trail from the shortcuts. A switchback might be little used, while a network of trails cutting straight up (and down) the mountain becomes the most heavily hiked path. But switchbacks don't just zigzag up a mountain to make the climb easier on hikers. They also keep the trail from eroding. Rain will follow a shortcut as the path of least resistance down a mountain, leaving an unsightly gully in its wake. Following the trail prevents this kind of erosion.

Hike Smart

Don't step on anything you can step over. Don't step over anything you can step around.

These are the first two rules of hiking, and they just may save your life. A rock on the trail seems innocent enough until it rolls out from under your foot. If you step *around* the obstacles you can, and step *over* the ones you can't step around, you can escape both the pain of a big accident and the embarrassment of a minor fall.

Maintain the Trail as You Hike

If you step over tree limbs in the trail, the person behind you will have to step over them too. When possible, take turns tossing limbs and sticks off the trail. The biggest trail-maintenance problem is litter. Nothing destroys the sensation of hiking in a wilderness faster than trash—even just an orange peel. Packing out your own trash isn't enough; pack out trash left by others too.

Equipment for a Day Hike

itting the trail without too many hassles is one of the best things about taking a short day hike. You don't need a lot of gear or preparation, but the gear you do take will be important. Wear comfortable clothes and sturdy hiking boots.

Make sure someone knows where you're going, what trail you'll be hiking, and when you plan to return. This will bring help faster if something goes wrong.

A map and a guidebook are listed as optional items but they're essential for hikes more than 2 miles long and on little-used or poorly marked trails. Most bookstores and backpacking shops carry a selection of books that describe hikes in the area. Never plan a hike longer than 10 miles in a single day. With the time it takes to get to the trail in the morning and back home at night, 10 miles of hiking makes a full day.

This minimum checklist does not include gear for all situations. A day hike to a high mountain peak, for example, would require as much equipment (though not as much food) as an overnight hike.

Day-Hike Checklist

One-liter (minimum) canteen
Rain gear (rain jacket and pants or poncho)
Food for the day
Lighter and waterproof matches
First aid kit (including bandages, moleskin)
Pocket knife
Bandana*

Toilet paper, trowel*
Map and compass*
Guidebook*
Camera and film*
Binoculars*
Gloves and knit cap+
Extra shirt or sweater*

+seasonal
* optional

Equipment for an Overnight Hike

The amount and type of equipment you pack for a trip will depend on where you are going. The snowy slopes of California's Sierra Nevadas call for different gear than you'd need on the Florida Trail. But the essentials will be the same no matter where you hike; it's the optional items that change. If possible, get recommendations from someone who has hiked in the area.

The less equipment you carry, the more comfortable your pack will be. After each trip, look through your gear as you unpack it. Anything you carried but never used is a candidate to stay at home next time. The only exceptions are the first aid kit and the other essentials.

Your Home on the Trail

Internal or external frame pack
Sleeping bag
Sleeping pad
Tent or tarp
Groundcloth*

+seasonal
*optional

Clothing

Light- or medium-weight
   hiking boots
Rain gear and pack cover
   (or trash bag)
Gaiters
1 pair of shorts
1 pair of loose-fitting
   long pants
1–2 short-sleeved shirts
1 long-sleeved shirt
1 sweater+
Hat and/or balaclava+
Down or synthetic-fill
   parka/vest+
2 pairs socks
2 pairs liner socks
1–2 bandanas
Long johns+
2 pairs underwear

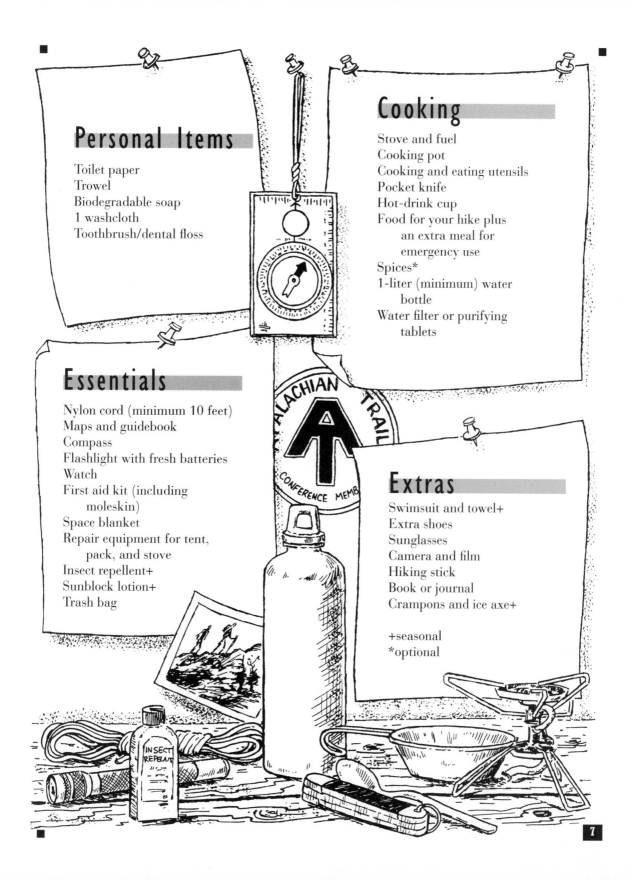

Personal Items

Toilet paper
Trowel
Biodegradable soap
1 washcloth
Toothbrush/dental floss

Cooking

Stove and fuel
Cooking pot
Cooking and eating utensils
Pocket knife
Hot-drink cup
Food for your hike plus
    an extra meal for
    emergency use
Spices*
1-liter (minimum) water
    bottle
Water filter or purifying
    tablets

Essentials

Nylon cord (minimum 10 feet)
Maps and guidebook
Compass
Flashlight with fresh batteries
Watch
First aid kit (including
    moleskin)
Space blanket
Repair equipment for tent,
    pack, and stove
Insect repellent+
Sunblock lotion+
Trash bag

Extras

Swimsuit and towel+
Extra shoes
Sunglasses
Camera and film
Hiking stick
Book or journal
Crampons and ice axe+

+seasonal
*optional

Hiking Pace

I t's easy to walk at a speed of 4 miles per hour around a track, but that pace would be hard to keep up for long in the mountains. Most people hike about 2½ miles per hour, so if you want to hike 10 miles in a day, you'll need 4 hours for hiking. That doesn't count the time for taking breaks, eating lunch, or watching wildlife.

Another way to look at pace is how far you travel with each stride. In the days of the Roman Empire, a thousand strides of the average Roman soldier was 5,280 times the length of his foot. That distance was known as a thousand paces, or *millia passuum* in Latin, and we now call it a mile.

A pace is still a good unit of measure to know. You can use your pace to determine distances and to navigate with a map and a compass. When hiking with a group, the person with the shortest pace should lead. It's much easier for hikers with longer strides to adjust their pace down than for hikers with shorter strides to walk faster. Following this practice will make for more enjoyable group hikes.

American Discovery Trail:
6,300 miles or
15,653,647 steps

How Many Steps?

Each pace is two steps. So, if your pace is 4 feet, you cover a little more than 2 feet with each step. At that pace, a 10-mile hike is 24,847 steps. Want to go on a longer hike? Try these:

Pacific Crest Trail:
2,600 miles or
6,460,235 steps

Appalachian Trail:
2,150 miles or
5,342,118 steps

To figure out how many steps you'll take on a particular trail at your pace:

1. Multiply the length of the trail in miles by 5,280 to get its length in feet. Example: 2,150 x 5,280 = 11,352,000 feet.
2. Divide that number by your pace length to get the number of paces. Example: 11,352,000 ÷ 4.25 = 2,671,059 paces.
3. Multiply the number of paces by 2 to determine the number of steps. Example: 2,671,059 x 2 = 5,342,118 steps.

Determining your hiking pace

Here's a simple way to figure out your hiking pace.

Measure out 100 feet on the ground. Now walk the distance at a natural pace—don't try to go slow or fast. Count each time your right foot comes down as you go. Do this a couple of times. The count should be about the same each time.

To determine your pace length, divide 100 by the number of paces you counted. For example, if your right foot came down 22 times, that would be 100 divided by 22, which is 4.54 or about 4½ feet per pace.

Water

Your body runs on water. Food is essential, but you *could* go without eating on a weekend backpacking trip if you had to. Without water you can live for only three or four days. At home, this is no problem—soda, juice, milk, and water are almost constantly available. In the backcountry, water sources can be 20 miles apart, making water a precious commodity.

How Much to Carry

For most backpacking trips you need to carry at least 1 liter of water. A source of water will be available at your camp and you can resupply there. If the weather is hot and dry, or if you usually drink a lot at home, you should carry 2 liters of water.

If you have to carry water to a dry camp, you should bring 1 gallon for a solo hiker. Groups should have 2 full liters of water per hiker and a spare gallon to prepare a meal and clean up.

Dehydration

When you're exerting yourself, your body *might* warn you that it's thirsty, but don't count on it. As you become dehydrated, your body's thirst indicators go on the blink. To avoid dehydration, make sure you drink plenty of water before you set out on the hike. A good rule to follow is: Drink as much as you can, and then drink that much again. And take a good gulp of water at every break during the hike.

The best way to tell if you're dehydrated is to check the color of your urine: Dark gold urine is a sign of dehydration. Drink lots of fluids to rehydrate your body, but steer clear of coffee, tea, and soft drinks that contain caffeine (such as Coke, Pepsi, and Mountain Dew). Caffeine will make you urinate more often and become more dehydrated.

What to Carry Water In

A 1-liter (or 1-quart) canteen is a good size for backpacking. It will carry all the water you need on the trail for most hikes and it can easily be stashed in a pack or carried in a pouch on your pack's hip belt. Wide-mouthed plastic bottles have replaced traditional canteens as a standard piece of backpacking gear. The wide mouth makes it easy to pour in powdered drink mix.

If you have a canteen with a carrying strap, use the canteen but forget the strap. A bottle of water dangling around your neck makes for an uncomfortable walk. Store it in your daypack or backpack, preferably in an outside pocket for easy access. If your hiking partners know where your water bottle is, they can reach it for you so you can keep your pack on.

Where Does the Water Go?

Your body loses water four ways at once:

Activity	Average Loss	Extremes
Respiration	1–2 liters per day	6 liters in cold or high altitude
Perspiration	1–2 liters per day	1–2 liters per hour when hot and dry
Urination	1–2 liters per day	0–4 liters depending on how you drink
Defecation	.1 liter per day	Up to 25 liters per day with diarrhea

"Dreamily, deliriously, I waded into waist-deep water and fell on my face....I had no fear of drowning in the water—I intended to drink it all."
—Edward Abbey, *Desert Solitaire*

Treating Water

Treating water only becomes an issue if you are camping or hiking in the backcountry. Established campgrounds, and even most primitive group camps, have a source of pure water. If you are on a backpacking trip, make sure you carry a liter or two of tap water or bottled water with you when you begin. You can quickly and easily treat water collected at rest stops and in camp.

The image of bending over a cool, clear spring and drinking from cupped hands is a romantic one, but these days that innocent-looking water is just as likely to contain *Giardia lamblia* and other bacteria and viruses. Drinking untreated water can trash your insides and produce symptoms like stomach cramps, diarrhea, fever, vomiting, fatigue, and eventually weight loss.

More than 120,000 cases of giardiasis alone are reported each year in the United States, and that doesn't count the cases that aren't reported or are misdiagnosed. If you use a little common sense and one of the following water-treatment methods, chances are you'll escape the ravages that can be caused by bad water.

Suspect water should always be treated; don't assume that a spring is OK just because it flows freely through the center of a wilderness area. A short distance up the slope from that beautiful spring there could lurk the remains of the last backpacker's toilet; if not a backpacker, maybe a bighorn sheep. In other words, there ain't no telling.

Boiling

Boiling is a simple but inconvenient way to treat water. Bring the water to a rolling boil to kill any disease organisms. The main drawback to this method is having to wait for the water to cool if it's already steamy outside.

Chemical Treatment

A chemical water-treatment system is more convenient but it gives a less-tasty end product. You can buy iodine water purifiers at outdoor supply stores. Read and carefully follow the instructions on the package. Iodine purifies 1 liter of water per tablet in about half an hour.

The drawback of iodine is its unpleasant aftertaste. You can mask the taste somewhat with powdered drink mix or you can buy a two-step iodine purifier; one tablet purifies and a second tablet of vitamin C clears the water of iodine taste. This system just takes extra time.

Water Filters

There is yet another option: water filters. A filter is the most reliable way to screen out giardiasis and other waterborne diseases, as long as its pores are small enough. Make sure your filter has a pore size of 1 micron or less. A pore size of more than 6 microns (or micrometers) will remove giardia cysts, which can be as large as 10 micrometers, but it won't remove other bacterial and viral organisms.

A variety of micropore water filters is available through outdoor retailers. Some filters also have an iodine chamber to chemically treat the water as they filter it; this kind of filter removes bacteria and viruses as well.

Cold-Weather Water Tips

Insulate your water by burying it in the snow. A lidded pot full of water will not freeze if it's buried at least a foot deep in snow. Just remember to mark where you've buried your water!

You can keep your bottle full of water by topping it off with snow each time you drink and shaking the bottle to mix in the snow.

Insulate your water bottle with an old foam pad and wrap it with duct tape.

Melting snow for water can burn a lot of fuel. A wind screen will boost your stove's heat output and speed up the process.

You can melt the snow more quickly if you pour about an inch of water into your cookpot before adding the snow.

Crusty, icy and wet snow produce more water than dry, powdery snow.

Keep your water liquid by stashing your water bottle deep within your sleeping bag as you hike. At night, stow the bottle in the toe end of your sleeping bag to keep the water from freezing. If this isn't possible, store the bottle upside down. That way, if it starts to freeze it will freeze at the "bottom" first and you'll still be able to get at your water.

"Watch out where the huskies go, and don't you eat that yellow snow." We all know to steer clear of "yellow" snow but the same goes for "pink" or "watermelon" snow. This snow also smells and tastes like watermelon but it hosts a microorganism that can give you stomach cramps and diarrhea.

Never drink ice water or "eat" snow when you're camping or hiking in the winter. The cold water will lower your core body temperature. Instead, hold the snow or water in your mouth until it's warm and then swallow it.

Make a solar still

A dry canteen in the parched landscape of the southwest United States and other dry regions is a serious problem. A thin sheet of plastic tucked in your pack can save your life on a summer desert trip. The solar still distills water from the soil and plant matter into your water bottle, producing about a pint of water in 3 hours.

Dig a hole 2 feet deep by 3 feet wide.
Set a wide-mouthed bottle in the bottom of the hole. Fill the area around the bottle with any green plant material you can find—leaves, grass, cactus, or whatever—cut or ripped to reveal the green insides.
Cover the hole with plastic (clear or translucent, if possible).

Weigh down the edges of the plastic around the hole to seal it.
Place a lightweight rock in the center of the plastic to form a funnel shape over the mouth of the bottle. Water will drip from the funnel into the bottle. You can insulate the sun-baked rock with a bandana to keep it from melting the plastic.

The heat of the sun cooks the plants and soil under the plastic to evaporate the water they contain. The water condenses on the plastic and drips down into the water container. It takes about 2 hours for the trapped air in the still to saturate with water enough to begin collecting in the water bottle.

Camp Stoves and Fuel

It's hard to deny the appeal of a campfire. Unfortunately, a fire is unreliable for cooking food. It's difficult to light a fire in wet weather and impossible in the driving rain. Fires aren't allowed in some parks and they're prohibited when the fire-hazard level is high. And they go against "leave-no-trace" camping ethics because no matter how careful you are, it's impossible to remove all signs of a fire.

Camp stoves are a great alternative. They come in various sizes, from lightweight backpacking stoves to three-burner camp models. Most packable camping stoves cost from $40 to $80.

No matter which stove you choose, try it out at home first. Cook a meal in your backyard so you can learn your stove's idiosyncrasies before you have to depend on it as your only way to cook.

The most commonly used fuels in the United States are white gas, butane, and propane.

White Gas Stoves

White gas (commonly sold as Coleman fuel) is the pick for many campers because it burns hot and clean and isn't as volatile as auto gas. Two- and three-burner white-gas camp stoves are a longtime favorite with big groups and car campers. For backpackers a single-burner white-gas (or multifuel) stove is the standard.

Most white-gas stoves need to be primed before lighting. This is a simple procedure but with some stoves it takes a little practice to get the hang of it. Always carefully read and follow the instructions that come with the stove.

Auto Gas

Auto gas is highly volatile. It contains additives that leave deposits in the fuel line and workings of the stove, making it necessary to clean your stove often. When you buy auto gas for your stove, get the lowest available octane rating.

All stoves that burn auto gas also burn white gas and many also burn kerosene. For best results use white gas whenever possible, even if your stove can take auto gas.

Butane and Propane

The greatest advantage of butane and propane is that they're easy to use. Bottled-gas stoves never need priming; just turn the knob and light the burner to get immediate maximum heat output.

The main drawback of these fuels is their containers. The bottles aren't refillable, which makes this form of fuel an environmentally bad choice. Butane fuel canisters can't be shipped by mail or taken on airplanes. Because of transportation laws, propane bottles are made of thick, heavy metal—too heavy for backpacking use.

Butane does not work well in cold temperatures. To combat this problem some manufacturers offer fuels blended from butane and propane. Blended-fuel stoves perform better in cold weather but they're still a poor choice for winter camping.

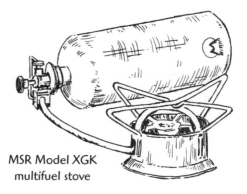

MSR Model XGK
multifuel stove

Other Fuel

Kerosene and denatured alcohol are the fuels of choice in Europe and you will occasionally see stoves in the United States made for these fuels. Kerosene is hard to clean up if it spills (other fuels evaporate quickly) and it's smoky when lit. Its heat output is good but the stove must be well primed to avoid stove-clogging soot. Alcohol is the least volatile fuel but it produces only about half the heat of white gas.

Forced-air wood camp stoves burn wood or charcoal and can be used in areas designated for stoves only because the fire is contained in a safe burner bowl.

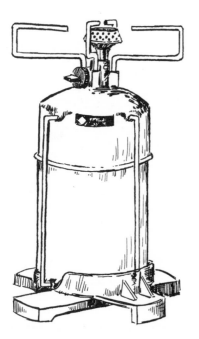

Camping Gaz Bleuet blended-fuel stove

The Bottom Line on Fuel

Testing one stove model with two different fuels for 50 hours of use, the Coleman Company made the following cost comparison:

White Gas: $45.00
Propane: $172.00

Make a buddy burner

A buddy burner provides fuel for the homemade camp-stove described in the next project. It's also a good idea to make one at home ahead of time so you'll have it on hand if you find yourself in the backcountry with a malfunctioning stove. Unfortunately, the smoke produced by this fuel is very black so it should be used in open areas only.

You will need:

a shallow tin can (such as a tuna can)

a 2-foot strip of corrugated cardboard just a little narrower than the height of the can

a tin can (such as a soup can or coffee can) containing paraffin wax

a lid from a larger can

a pot of water on the stove

Fair warning:
Unless you want to be grounded from now until you retire, don't try melting the wax until you clear it with your parents. This project can be messy if you're not careful.

1. Roll the cardboard into a coil that will fit loosely in the shallow tin can.
2. Set the can of paraffin into the pot of water on the stove.
3. Melt the paraffin slowly over low heat. If the vapor given off by the paraffin catches on fire, use the lid from the larger can to smother the flames.

4. Pour the melted paraffin over the cardboard coil in the shallow tin can. The can should be filled nearly to the top with melted paraffin.
5. Let the paraffin harden. The buddy burner is now ready.

You can use sawdust instead of cardboard to make a buddy burner. Just fill the shallow tin can with sawdust and pour the melted paraffin over it.

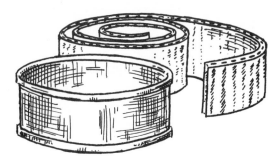

To use your buddy burner, light the fuel with a match and place your homemade stove over the burner. When you're finished cooking, lift off the camp stove and "turn off" the burner by smothering the flames with a large can or pot lid or even with the bottom of the pan you're cooking in.

Remember to use a pot holder to lift the stove, or a stick to knock it over, because it will be very hot. The paraffin will be a hot liquid that sticks to the skin—wait for it to harden again before moving the burner.

Make your own camp stove

This camp stove can be used with the buddy burner you made in the previous project.

You will need:

> a large tin can (such as a coffee can)
> a pair of tin snips
> a punch-style can opener
> a hammer
> work gloves

1. The closed end of the can will serve as the top of your stove. Wearing your gloves, use the tin snips to cut a door in the stove. From the open end, cut two slits about 3 inches long and 3 inches apart. Bend the flap of tin backward into the can and hammer it flat.

2. Punch two or three small holes near (not on!) the closed end of the can, on the side opposite the door. The holes are used to vent the smoke produced by the buddy burner.

To use the stove, find a level spot outdoors so the food won't spill over the side of the pot while it cooks. If you can't find a level spot, use a twig or a small dry stone to level the pot. A wet stone might explode from the heat of the stove.

Now place the stove over a buddy burner. You can use a small twig fire instead, keeping it small but steadily burning. Use the door to fuel the twig fire.

The first time you use your stove, the finish will melt off the can. Hold the closed end with a pot holder and wipe the can with a paper towel. If you have trouble with smoke forming a black deposit on the can, try coating the stove with liquid soap before each use. This will make the stove easy to clean after cooking.

Cooking

After a day outdoors you'll be ready for a good meal. For canoeists, cyclists, and backpackers, supper time means pulling out a one-pot wonder. Campers can enjoy the added luxury of a two-burner stove or more than one stove. Either way, a bad meal probably won't ruin a great day, but a tasty dinner sure can cheer you up on a cold, wet day.

Your first choice is whether to opt for the prefabricated concoctions offered in backpacking shops or to head for the supermarket.

Supermarket Food

All the food you need for the backcountry is no farther away than your supermarket. The pasta, rice, eggs, vegetables, and meat you eat at home make great meals in camp too. From the backpacker's mainstay of macaroni and cheese, to camp stew, it is all less expensive than the prepackaged food mentioned above. The drawbacks are that supermarket food is generally heavier and bulkier, and a green pepper or pound of hamburger won't keep long on the trail.

Freeze-Dried Meals

There is a wide variety of one-, two-, and four-person freeze-dried meals, from Hawaiian chicken to beans and rice. These meals are expensive too, but because they're lightweight, easy to prepare, and often tasty, you might want to have at least one with you on every trip. Freeze-dried food makes a good emergency supply to stash in your pack in case you have to spend an unexpected extra night in the woods. And it's perfect for those nights when you're too tired to cook a complicated dinner.

Precooked Meals

A precooked backpacking meal offers the ultimate in convenience. It comes in a foil pouch that you simply heat and serve (or tear open and eat if you don't mind cold food). These meals are heavy and expensive but they're great for the culinarily impaired.

Pots and Utensils

The minimum in cookware for a solo trip is one 2-quart pot with a lid and a handle, a cup, a spoon, and a pocket knife. A second, smaller pot would be the next piece of equipment to add. Two nesting pots and a lid are easy to carry, and you'll have one pot for your meal and another to boil water for a hot drink.

When you travel with someone else you'll also want a bowl to eat from. The second person can carry a Teflon frying pan and a spatula for making toast, pancakes, and grilled sandwiches. For four or more campers a 4-quart pot and a hefty wooden spoon make it easier to cook big meals. Groups may want to carry some or all of these items as well: measuring cup, mixing bowl, cutting board, grater, tongs, pot holders, strainer, coffee pot, steak knives, and a cast-iron Dutch oven. What you take will depend on your menu, the size of your group, and the length of your trip.

Packing Food for the Backcountry

Space and weight are always a concern on backpacking, canoeing, or bike camping trips. To cut down on the bulk of your food supplies, take rice, pasta, and prepared foods out of their cardboard boxes and pack them into resealable plastic bags of appropriate sizes. Small packets, such as the powdered cheese in a macaroni and cheese mix, can be slipped unopened into the bag with the rest of the mix. If you need the instructions for a packaged meal, cut out that portion of the box and include it in the same bag.

Be sure to seal powders such as dried milk in twist-tie bags before packing them in resealable bags; powder will clog the "zipper" of a resealable bag and makes it leak.

Fun Recipes

As we near the next millennium, food choices for campers can be as technologically advanced as something dreamed up in a 1950s science fiction movie. But do we *really* want dehydrated ice cream or military-style MREs (meals ready to eat) while we enjoy the great outdoors?

Here are some recipes that have been old standbys for campers for the past century and will no doubt be popular well into the next.

S'mores

This is the all-time favorite camping dessert. You will need:

    Chocolate bars, broken into squares
    Graham crackers
    Marshmallows

1. Break a cracker in half and place a square of chocolate on one half.
2. Toast a marshmallow over the campfire or grill fire until it's golden brown (or darker).
3. Place it over the chocolate, top it with the other half of cracker, gently press it all together, and munch away.

Tired of the same ol', same ol'? Try using:

peanut butter or toasted peanuts instead of chocolate to make Robinson Crusoes

slices of apples instead of crackers to make Apple S'mores

chocolate-covered graham crackers and no chocolate bars

chocolate peppermint patties instead of chocolate bars

G.O.R.P. or Gorp

The name stands for Good Ol' Raisins and Peanuts. You can make this time-honored trail snack to suit your own tastes. Mix your choice of the following ingredients and feel free to add your own.

  Peanuts and/or other nuts
  Raisins (plain, chocolate, and/or yogurt-
    covered)
  M&Ms (plain, peanut, and/or almond)
  Cheerios or other cereal
  Chopped dried fruit
  Shredded coconut
  Reese's Pieces
  Sunflower seeds

Campfire Stew

Try this awesome meal the first day of hiking so the hamburger doesn't go bad. Serves 6–8. You will need:

  2 pounds hamburger
  1 onion, peeled and diced
  2 cans condensed vegetable soup
  Salt and pepper

1. Add salt and pepper to the hamburger and mix thoroughly.
2. Roll pieces of hamburger into small balls.
3. Cook the hamburger with the onion in a large pot over the campfire or on a camp stove. Cook until the onion is translucent and the hamburger is well browned.
4. If necessary, pour off the excess fat, dig a "cat hole" well away from camp, and carefully bury the fat.
5. Add the vegetable soup and enough water to keep it from sticking.
6. Cover and cook slowly for at least 20 minutes to cook the meat through. Serve hot.

Tomato Sunrise

This belly-warming breakfast will serve 6–8. You will need:

  2½ tablespoons margarine
  2½ tablespoons flour
  3 cans condensed tomato soup
  ½ pound cheddar cheese, cut in small
    cubes
  16 slices toast
  Salt and pepper

1. Toast bread on sticks over the campfire or on the grill.
2. Melt the margarine slowly in a large pot over low heat.
3. Add the flour to the margarine and mix until all the lumps are gone.
4. Add the cans of soup and stir until heated through.
5. Gently stir in the cheese until it melts.
6. Add salt and pepper to taste.
7. Serve the Tomato Sunrise over toast.

Damper or Ash Bread, Twists, and Bannocks

These recipes use a standard biscuit dough. Use your favorite recipe or try the following:

    4 cups all-purpose flour
    1 teaspoon salt
    ¼ cup dry skim milk
    8 teaspoons baking powder
    ¾ stick margarine
    1 cup cold water

1. Thoroughly mix the dry ingredients.
2. Cut in the margarine until the mixture looks like coarse cornmeal. Do not mix in the margarine until just before you hit the trail.
3. Store the mixture in a tough plastic bag or a waterproof food bag.
4. When you're ready to make the dough, add the full amount of water to the bag, or dump the flour mix into a bowl and add the water.
5. Stir until the dough forms a ball.

To make damper or ash bread:

1. Pat biscuit dough into a flat loaf about 1 inch thick.
2. Cover both sides of the loaf with large leaves.
3. Push aside coals (and ashes, if using a wood fire).
4. Lay the leaf-wrapped dough on the hot ground and cover it with coals (and ashes).
5. Bake 10 minutes.
6. Push a straw into the bread to test it. If the straw comes out clean, the bread is done.

To make twist bread:

1. Find a stick about 2 feet long and 2 inches thick (use only downed wood) and peel off the bark.
2. Preheat the stick by the fire or grill.
3. Wet the stick.
4. Roll out a long "snake" of dough and twist it around the stick.
5. Push the end of the stick into the ground so that the dough can bake over the fire or grill.
6. Turn the stick often and reverse it if necessary to brown the dough evenly. The bread is ready to eat when it is completely browned.

To make bannock bread:

1. Form the dough into a 1-inch-thick loaf that will fit into your frying pan. Don't grease the pan.
2. Bake for 7 to 8 minutes over coals to brown the bottom of the bread.
3. Tilt the pan nearly vertical in front of a bright fire to brown the top of the bread. This should take another 7 to 8 minutes.

Orange- or Onion-Coddled Eggs

You will need half an orange or half an onion for each egg you wish to bake.

1. Choose either an orange or an onion to use as a shell. Clean the fruit from half an orange or remove all but about three of the outer layers from half a large onion.
2. Crack an egg into your preferred shell.
3. Set the shell in the coals and cook until the egg is done.
4. Eat your coddled egg right from the shell. You can eat the onion shell as well if you removed the outer, scorched layer first.

Foil Dinner

This is a delicious and easy-to-make meal. For each person you will need:

> One hamburger patty
> One potato, peeled or scrubbed and cubed
> One carrot, peeled or scrubbed and cut in strips
> One onion, peeled and cut in wedges
> Salt and pepper
> Aluminum foil

1. Place a hamburger patty on a large piece of tinfoil.
2. Cover the hamburger with the vegetables.
3. Sprinkle with salt and pepper to taste.
4. Fold over the foil and close it securely to make a small, tight package.
5. Place the package in coals and cook for 15 to 30 minutes, depending on the heat of the coals.

Baked Fruit

Another foil-wrapped recipe with delicious results. You will need one apple or banana per person.

1. Core the apple or slice the banana down the center.
2. Stuff the fruit with your choice of sugar, cinnamon, chocolate chips, marshmallows, or nuts. Or try them all!
3. Wrap securely in foil and place the package in hot coals.
4. Bake the apple for 30 minutes, the banana for no more than 15 minutes.

Cleaning Up After Meals

As soon as you finish eating, it's time to clean up your pots, pans, and dishes. This keeps food from drying to them and discourages animals, like raccoons and mice, who love to lick scraps off pots and dishes. If you have much leftover food you should pack it out in a resealable plastic bag.

When you've scraped the food out of your big cookpot, pour in a splash of water to rinse the dishes and other pots in. Rub with your fingers to get off most or even all the visible bits of food. If you're having trouble getting off any food stuck to the pot, take out the pot scrubber and work until it gleams again. There should be very little food content in the water. You can

scatter this water well away from camp and any water source.

Pour a cup of water into your cookpot (more if you are washing dishes for a group). Heat this water on the cook stove. You don't have to bring it to or near a boil; just get the water good and hot. Add a little biodegradable soap and wash the dishes and pans in this pot. When all the dishes and cookware are clean, carry them well away from camp and at least 200 yards from any water source. Dump out the soapy water and rinse off all the pots and dishes. If the water source for your campsite is questionable, use only boiled or filtered water for this final rinse.

Tents

There are four main points to consider when you try to distinguish among the myriad tents you'll find in stores and catalogues: shape, capacity, whether the tent is freestanding, and the number of seasons it's made for. As with all equipment, which tent is right for you depends on how you want to use it. The perfect tent for base camp on Mount Everest would obviously be the wrong choice for a family overnighting at a private campground.

A-Frame

When you think of a tent, the traditional A-frame may be the first one that comes to mind. This tent is not freestanding but requires numerous tent pegs to hold it upright. The steep-sloping sides stand up well against the wind but reduce the headroom inside. A-frame tents are usually inexpensive.

The *modified A-frame* tent has two poles at each end connected to a main ridge support. These extra poles make the tent freestanding.

Tunnel

A tunnel tent is supported by a large hoop at the entrance and an equal-size or smaller hoop at the foot. Its shape makes it roomier than an A-frame of the same size, and it's a popular choice for backpackers because it tends to be lightweight and easy to pitch. However, the tunnel tent is rarely freestanding and in heavy winds it must be pitched with the foot of the tent facing into the wind.

A variation known as the *hoop tent* features three hoops, often equal in size. Resembling a covered wagon, this tent is larger and roomier than the regular tunnel tent but it sheds wind poorly.

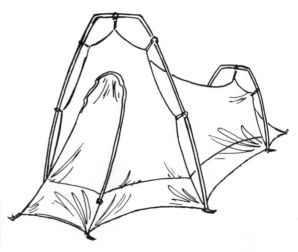

Dome

Freestanding and roomy, the six-sided dome tent is made in sizes ranging from two-person back-packing models to big family tents. Each offers the maximum living space for a given floor size. The hexagonal shape creates an extra triangle of floor space on either side of the rectangular sleeping area–great places to store your gear.

When you choose a dome tent, be sure that its rainfly has a vestibule or extends well out over the doorway. A rainfly is the protective outside cover that does the real job of blocking out rain. The roof of the tent itself is usually made with a lighter fabric to aid ventilation. Without a fly, rain will fall into the tent when you come and go. Tentmakers have created a number of spin-off designs that use the three arched poles of the dome tent. The rectangular floor and the tapered hexagon are two common variations. Tapering the tent from the entrance to the foot makes it more lightweight and wind resistant.

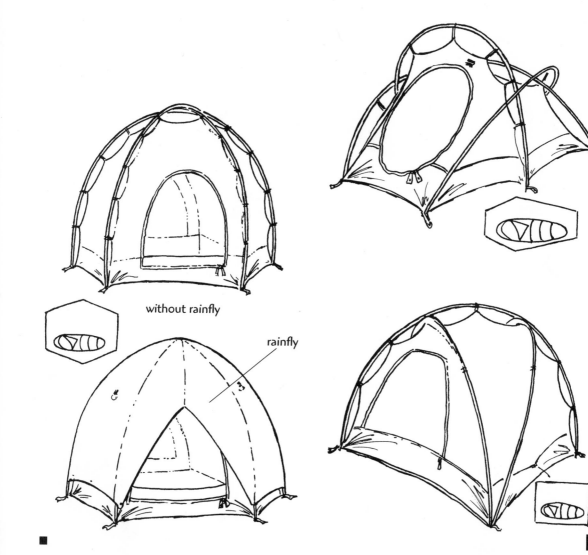

without rainfly

rainfly

Cabin

These large, vertical-walled tents made for car camping are popular with families. Some cabin tents feature a screened porch, a large awning, or a divider that creates two rooms.

Umbrella

Also known as a square dome, the umbrella tent is a cross between a dome tent and a cabin tent. It has near-vertical walls and two or three poles crossing over the ceiling to give lots of headroom. It's freestanding like a dome tent but as easy to stand up in as a cabin tent. This heavy tent is also made for car camping.

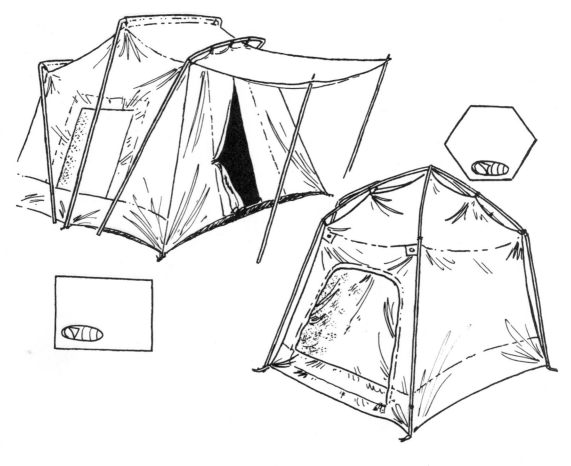

Tent Capacity

Tentmakers rate their tents by the number of people that they can comfortably sleep. This number is based on an average person with an average amount of gear and is often an optimistic estimate. A two-person tent will hold two people, but doesn't always leave room for any gear. The best way to get a feel for the size of a tent is to set it up and climb inside. Picture the number of people who will be in the tent and how much gear they will have. Lie down and see how much room remains at the head and foot of the tent and how much on either side.

Freestanding Tents

Self-supporting and easy to set up, move, and clean, freestanding tents are offered by almost every tentmaker. Their long support poles make them heavier than staked tents of the same size. Freestanding tents should be staked immediately or filled with gear; otherwise, they will blow away in just a stout breeze. Even when they are full of people and gear they should be staked down if stormy weather is expected.

Seasons

Tents are built to fit various seasons and climates. *Summer* tents have lots of netting to provide ventilation and they rely on a nylon floor and rainfly to keep out the rain. They are made for drier weather and lighter winds.

Most tents are for *three-season* use; they will shed heavy rain and all but heavy winds. A three-season tent often has a breathable canopy covered by a waterproof rainfly that extends to within a few inches of the ground. The tent itself should have adequate ventilation so that moisture won't condense inside. These tents fit the needs of most campers and backpackers.

Four-season tents have stronger poles to take the stresses of high winds and snow. The floor has a high rise that creates a bathtub shape for keeping out splashing mud and wind-driven rain. The rainfly often has a vestibule, like a low covered porch, that creates a sheltered kitchen space outside the entrance. The rainfly is often brightly colored to make the tent easy to spot in the snow.

Weight

A tent's weight is an important factor in choosing a tent for backpacking. A good rule of thumb is that a backpacking tent should weigh no more than 3 to 4 pounds per person (and the less the better). Most tentmakers shave ounces or even pounds off their backpacking tents by tapering the height from the front entrance to the foot. This gives you enough room to change clothes or play cards without adding material where it isn't needed.

When you share a tent with another hiker you'll want to split the weight as well: One person carries the tent while the other carries a comparable amount of cooking gear and food.

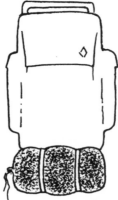
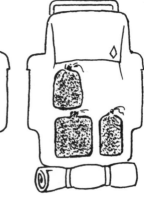

9-pound, three-person tent

2-pound, one-person tent

Seal the Tent Seams

New tents are not waterproof until you seal the seams. Set up your new tent and rainfly at home and let it sit for 3 or 4 hours before you begin sealing the seams. This will let the needle holes you are sealing extend to their maximum size. Remove the rainfly and seal all its seams first, following the manufacturer's recommendations. At least one manufacturer recommends sealing exterior seams as well. If the tent's floor seams were not factory sealed, you will have to seal them now.

Groundcloths

A sheet of polyethylene between the tent and the ground will protect the floor of the tent from punctures. The groundsheet should be slightly smaller than your tent to keep it from channeling the water under the tent. If you always use a groundcloth you'll not only keep drier in wet weather but extend the life of your tent as well.

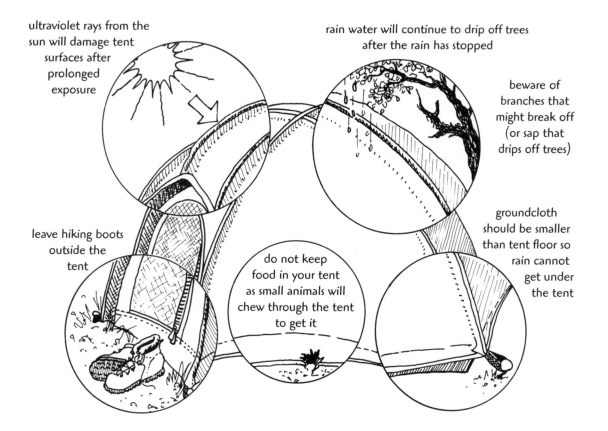

ultraviolet rays from the sun will damage tent surfaces after prolonged exposure

rain water will continue to drip off trees after the rain has stopped

beware of branches that might break off (or sap that drips off trees)

leave hiking boots outside the tent

do not keep food in your tent as small animals will chew through the tent to get it

groundcloth should be smaller than tent floor so rain cannot get under the tent

Caring for Your Tent

Sun and moisture are the two main elements your tent protects you from (along with bugs). And they're also your tent's worst enemies.

Prolonged exposure to the ultraviolet rays of the sun will degrade the fabric and waterproofing of your tent. You should only leave your tent pitched when you intend to use it.

To keep moisture from forming mildew in your tent, dry out a wet tent as soon as possible by setting it up in the sun. When you get home from a camping trip, always set up your tent and let it air out. Freestanding tents can be set up and then hung from a tree.

Two other ways to extend the life of your tent are to remove your boots before getting into the tent and to pitch your tent away from fires, stoves, and other sources of heat. Pets can also wear out tent floors quickly. Store food outside the tent to keep curious animals from tearing their way through the fabric to find a meal.

Tarps

A tarp is a lightweight and inexpensive alternative to a tent. The main drawback to a tarp is that it doesn't keep the bugs out. There are areas of this great country of ours that are absolutely unbearable during certain seasons. The blackflies in New England are as notorious as gnats in the South and sand fleas along the coasts. The names vary but the "monsters" are drawn the same—large pointed teeth in a body that is all mouth. If you intend to use a tarp, make sure you have a sleep screen for bug season.

Buying tarps can be tricky. The idea behind them is light weight at low cost but in some cases they can weigh as much and cost as much as a good backpacking tent. Your best bet is to purchase either a translucent white polyethylene sheet or a coated nylon sheet. Polyethylene is cheaper but it decays faster in the sun than coated nylon.

Sizes vary but the best size is 10 feet by 12 feet. Another thing to check is whether the tarp has grommets for you to attach your ropes to. If it doesn't, you'll have to purchase or jury-rig some clamps. You can wrap small stones at the corners of the tarp, securing the material above it with a rope, or purchase the popular Visklamp to secure the tarp to a length of rope.

To set up a tarp, you will need to purchase:

50 feet of ¼-inch braided nylon rope for the tarp's ridge line
100 feet of ⅛-inch braided nylon rope for guy-lines
6 to 8 tent pegs to secure the tarp in case there are no rocks, roots, trees, or bushes available
cloth tape or a tent repair kit

Shed-Roof Tarp

This is the easiest way to rig a tarp because it requires only two trees reasonably close together.
1. Find two trees that are far enough apart for the tarp to fit easily between them.
2. Lift one side of the tarp 6 to 8 feet off the ground and attach one corner to each tree. Make sure it's facing away from the wind.
3. With the low side of the tarp facing into the wind, peg the two corners to the ground with tent stakes. If it is especially windy you may have to use another couple of stakes between the two corners to keep the tarp from flapping in the wind.

A-Frame Tarp

Another common tarp setup.
1. Find two trees at least ten feet apart.
2. Using your ridge line rope (50 feet), tie each end to a tree about 6 to 8 feet off the ground. Make sure the rope is taut so that the ridge line does not sag.
3. Drape the tarp over the rope in the shape of—surprise—an A-frame tent.

4. Stake the four corners of the tarp to the ground. Depending on the weather, you may want to vary how you stake the tarp. If it is on the warm side, leave some air space at the bottom for ventilation.

Modified A-Frame

If you are in an area where there are no trees or boulders to help you set up a tarp, try this version of the A-frame.
1. Find 4 makeshift poles—sound branches, driftwood, or whatever is handy—at least a few feet long.
2. Peg one end of the ridge line rope to the ground.
3. Make an A-fame shape with the first set of 2 poles.
4. Wrap the ridge line rope securely around the top of the A-frame where the poles cross.
5. From the first set of poles, extend the rope the width of the tarp (about 8 feet). Then lash the second set of 2 poles.

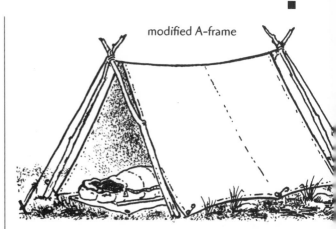

modified A-frame

6. Make sure the ridge line is taut between the poles before lashing the end of the line to a stake and stamping it into the ground.
7. Throw your tarp over the ridge line and stake the corners and edges as needed.

Tying Tent Guylines

To make an easy-to-adjust guyline for tent, tarp, and dining fly stakes, use a combination of two half-hitches and a taut-line hitch. Tie the two half-hitches to the grommet on the tent or fly. Tie the taut-line hitch to the stake end of the line. This will allow you to adjust the line after the stake is in the ground.

Hanging a Clothesline

If you have a 10-foot length of rope, look for two trees 8 feet or less apart to hang a clothesline. Tie a clove hitch to the first tree and two half-hitches with quick release to the second. This will hold up the line under the weight of wet clothes or a sleeping bag that needs airing out, but will be easy to untie.

If you have a long enough rope (15 to 20 feet) you can hang your clothes without clothes pins. Double the rope and twist it thoroughly. Tie the ends to two trees as before. To hang up your clothes, pull the two strands apart and tuck a corner of the garment in between them. Let go and the rope will snap back and hold on to the garment.

Sleeping Bags

You will spend about a third of your time on a camping trip in your sleeping bag, so getting the right bag is important. First you should select the proper shape, then consider the comfort rating, bulk, and weight of the bag.

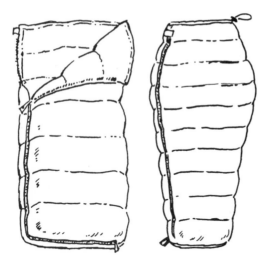

Rectangular

This is the roomiest and the heaviest of sleeping bags. Room and ventilation are also the rectangular bag's drawbacks on cold nights because there is more air to heat up and no hood to prevent heat from escaping through your head. It can make a convenient bedroll for cabin or tent camping in mild weather, but it's not the best choice for backpackers.

Semirectangular

This bag offers the tapered shape of a mummy bag but doesn't have a hood. The design cuts down on weight and provides good ventilation because it is zippered on three sides like a rectangular bag. It offers a good compromise between the roominess of a rectangular bag and the warmth of a mummy bag, but it is not designed for more than moderately cold weather (freezing and above).

Mummy

The form-fitting mummy bag leaves the least amount of extra air to warm. It also uses the least material, which trims the weight and makes it the best choice for backpackers. The hood can be drawn tight around your head in cold weather to cut back on heat loss. Most mummy bags also feature a "boxed" foot section that keeps the insulation in place over your feet so they stay warmer. Comfort ratings for mummy bags start at around 30 degrees and drop to well below freezing. This bag's only drawback is that it can be very confining—not much room to toss and turn at night. And if the weather turns mild, you'll roast!

Comfort Rating

Every sleeping bag has a comfort rating that gives the lowest temperature at which an average person will be comfortable in the bag. There is no standardized method for determining these numbers and they vary greatly from one manufacturer to another, so ratings will help you compare one sleeping bag to another only if they are made by the same company.

As a rule, a 20-degree bag is a good all-around bag for camping from early spring through late fall in most parts of the country. Winter campers should look for a 0-degree or even a −10-degree bag. A good cold-weather bag will also have a well-insulated draft tube covering the zipper.

How warm you are in your bag depends on more than the comfort rating of your bag, such as when and how much you last ate, what you wear to bed, the kind of sleeping pad you use, and the type of shelter you sleep in. Moisture trapped in your clothes during the day will keep you colder at night, so be sure to change clothes before you go to bed.

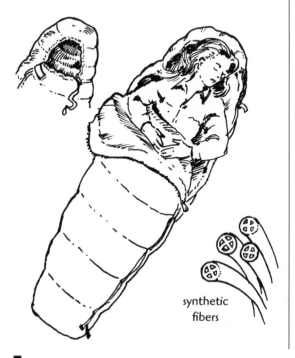

synthetic fibers

Insulation Material

Your bag's filling will determine how well it performs. Down bags last longer and keep you warmer than any synthetic. So why aren't all bags made out of down? Because sleeping in a wet down bag feels about as warm as lying in a puddle of water.

Synthetic fillings are well suited to wet climates and canoe camping because they retain a good percentage of their insulating ability when wet. They also dry out much more quickly than down. Most of these fillings use small, thin fibers bonded into fluffy masses.

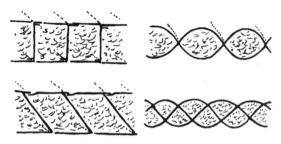

sleeping bag cross sections

No filling keeps you as warm when it's wet as when it's dry. To keep your sleeping bag dry even in a downpour, line the bag's stuff sack with a plastic garbage bag. Stuff the sleeping bag into the plastic bag inside the stuff sack and tie off the plastic bag. Close the stuff sack over the plastic bag and you can be confident that you'll have a dry bag at night.

Bulk and Weight

Car campers aren't limited by the dimensions of the sleeping bag compartment of an internal frame pack. But a backpacker needs a sleeping bag that fits the compartment and weighs less than 5 pounds. Many good bags can be found in the 2½- to 4½-pound range. The less a bag weighs for a given comfort rating, the more it will cost.

winter
sleeping bag

summer
sleeping bag

Caring for Your Bag

Your sleeping bag's warmth will be quickly diminished if you don't care for the bag properly. A bag loses its loft (its insulating thickness), and consequently its warmth, when it's packed tightly for long periods. Store your bag in a big, loose sack at home and save the small stuff sack for camping trips. Never roll your bag up to put it into a stuff sack. This curls the insulation the same way each time and creates cold pockets in the bag.

Synthetic bags can be machine washed in cold water with a mild detergent (such as Ivory). They should be dried on the lowest setting of your dryer, if not air dried. Down bags should be hand washed and air dried only. After you've air dried a down bag you can toss it in the dryer with a towel to absorb any remaining moisture. Be sure to use the lowest setting of the dryer and never let the bag get warm to the touch. Loosen the matted down with your fingers to help the bag regain its loft.

Bag Liners and Overbags

Not every bag is right for every trip. Instead of keeping a closet full of sleeping bags of different comfort ratings, you can get a bag liner. A liner can add as much as 20 degrees' insulation to your bag. It can also be used by itself on a hot summer night. If you don't have enough room inside your bag to fit a liner, you can get an overbag, which your sleeping bag fits inside, instead.

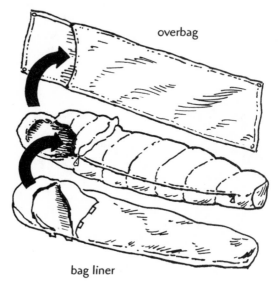

overbag

bag liner

Sleeping Pads

A sleeping pad is essential for sleeping warm and comfy outdoors. There are four main types of pads: closed-cell foam, open-cell foam, self-inflating, and air mattresses. Pads also come in different lengths. To cut back on weight for backpackers, all pads (except air mattresses) are available in three-quarter as well as full length. Winter campers will need the insulation of a full-length pad, but the three-quarter length is comfortable for most other camping situations.

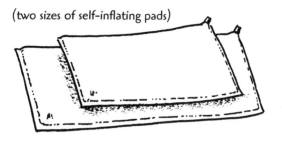

(two sizes of self-inflating pads)

A *self-inflating pad* is an open-cell foam pad wrapped in an air- and watertight nylon cover with an air valve. When you open the valve the pad "breathes" in air to fill out the pad's loft. To pack it away you open the valve and tightly roll up the pad. The self-inflater is double the weight of a closed-cell foam pad, but still lightweight and very cushy. You need to carry a patch kit in case your pad is punctured in the backcountry.

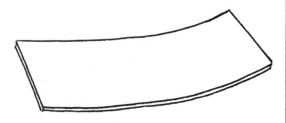

A *closed-cell foam pad*, made of dense polyethylene, is cheap and durable but bulky to pack, and it offers less padding than the others.

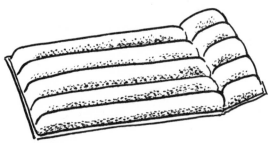

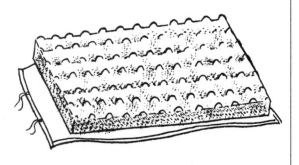

Open-cell foam pads are made of spongier polyurethane. They're light and they pack more tightly than closed-cell pads, but they soak up water like the sponges they resemble. To compensate they're sometimes sold with protective nylon covers.

Air mattresses are too bulky and heavy for backpackers, but they offer added comfort for car campers. They're useless if they get punctured, so you need a patch kit with this pad too.

Hiking Boots

If your feet are unhappy, you're unhappy. If you tried hiking over rough terrain in tennis shoes your feet would get very sore, because the sole of a tennis shoe bends with every rock or root on the trail. A good pair of hiking boots gives your feet the support and protection they need to transport you over the backcountry. Looking at boots in three weight categories helps sort out the many choices available.

Lightweight Boots

For backpacking and day hiking on mostly gentle terrain it's most important to have ankle support and soles that grip the trail. A whole crop of boots weighing under 2.5 pounds appeared about 10 years ago to fill this niche of the boot market. Today these fabric-and-leather boots, which sometimes look like high-top sneakers, can be seen everywhere—not just on trails but walking the malls and school hallways too.

Lightweight boots with fabric uppers get wet easily but they also dry out more quickly than their heavier counterparts. One feature to look for is a *fully gussetted tongue:* extra material connects the tongue to the upper, forming a seal to keep out dirt, twigs, and water. A synthetic *shank* in the sole offers extra support. Light boots are made of as much fabric as leather, so they don't need much breaking in.

Mediumweight Boots

These boots weigh from 2½ to 4 pounds, with leather (or mostly leather) uppers and sturdy lugged soles. They're good for day hiking or backpacking even on rough terrain, and their added ankle support makes rough hiking easier on your body. The sole should have a one-half- to three-quarter-length steel shank to keep it from giving in to every rock and root in the trail.

The fewer seams the uppers have, the better they'll keep out moisture. Leather boots will keep your feet dry longer in rain and mud, but they also take longer to dry out than light boots.

Mediumweight boots break in slowly as the leather learns to bend where your foot and ankle bend. This makes a good fit important, so try them on before you buy. If you order your boots by mail, first make sure you'll be able to return or exchange them if they don't fit just right.

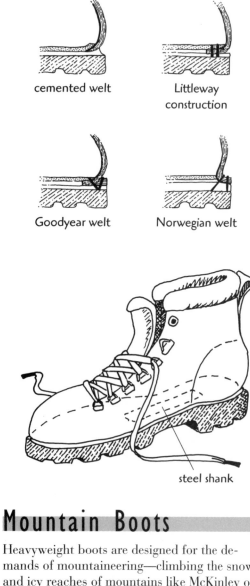

cemented welt

Littleway construction

Goodyear welt

Norwegian welt

steel shank

Mountain Boots

Heavyweight boots are designed for the demands of mountaineering—climbing the snowy and icy reaches of mountains like McKinley or even Everest. Most boots in this category are made for use with *crampons*, or spiked plates, on snow and alpine rock. They have a half- to full-length steel shank in a close-trimmed sole, and embedded crampon grooves and toe and heel protrusions for better crampon fit. Many heavyweight boots are made with stiff, thick leather; some have a molded plastic exterior with an insulating inner boot liner.

Fitting Boots

Even the best hiking boot will chew up your foot if it doesn't fit properly. If the boot is too tight it will contort your foot to fit its own shape, but a loose-fitting boot is a blister factory. The most important thing to remember when you try on boots is to wear the same sock combination you'll be wearing on the trail. And take your time in the store.

Start by getting your foot measured for size. Your boot size will not be the same as your shoe size for many brands. Pay attention to the width as well as the length. Boots come in several widths and this can make all the difference in how well they fit.

Try on boots made by several different manufacturers. Each bootmaker has a slightly different mold (called a *last*) that they build their boots around. One manufacturer's boot shape may fit your foot much better than another's.

Feel how the boot fits even before you lace it up. Before it's laced the boot should be snug, but not tight. Wiggle your toes. If they bump the toe of the boot, don't lace it up; try a half-size larger. When you've laced the boot, walk around the store—though the smooth, padded surface of a carpeted floor is the worst place to try the fit. Try walking on an incline to see if your foot slides to the front of the boot. This feels uncomfortable enough in the store, but it can be excruciating on a long downhill with a 35- to 45-pound pack on your back. Your boots should have a roomy toebox, though, to accommodate trail-swollen dogs.

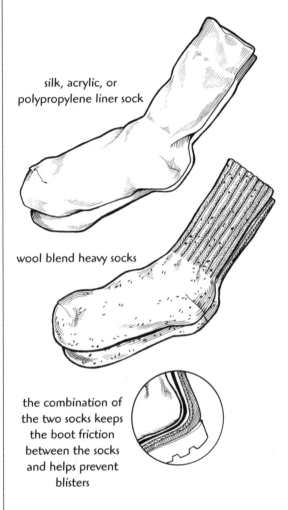

silk, acrylic, or polypropylene liner sock

wool blend heavy socks

the combination of the two socks keeps the boot friction between the socks and helps prevent blisters

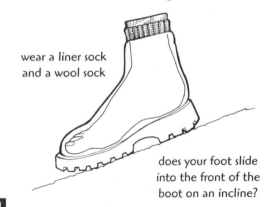

wear a liner sock and a wool sock

does your foot slide into the front of the boot on an incline?

Socks

Always wear two pairs of socks with hiking boots. A thin liner sock made out of silk, acrylic, or polypropylene can "wick" moisture away from your sweaty foot to keep you dry. A cushiony outer sock of wool or blended nylon, polypropylene, or another synthetic will keep your feet comfortable. This double layer of socks will help prevent blisters and is standard hiking wear.

when breaking in boots, wear a fully loaded pack for walking

Caring for Your Boots

All the leather in your boots will need waterproofing on a routine basis. Carefully follow the manufacturer's instructions for applying the waterproofing. The more you hike, the more often you will need to rewaterproof your boots.

Always clean the dirt out of your boots before waterproofing or packing them away after a trip. If they're wet, don't dry them by a fire or heater, which can melt the soles, loosen the glue, and be the death of a good pair of boots. When you get home you can dry them slowly in a cool, dry place. Stuffing bunched-up newspaper inside the boots can help absorb moisture. If it's been a particularly wet hike, clean and waterproof them again before packing them away.

Sprinkle foot powder into your boots before you put them on to keep moisture and odor to a minimum.

stuff shoe with newspapers to dry

Breaking In Boots

No matter which boots you buy, you'll have to break them in well before hitting the trail. Start by wearing them on short walks around your neighborhood. For lightweight boots a few short walks should be enough to prepare for a real hike. With leather boots the process takes a little more time, but a few more walks will get them ready for short hikes. Pick up some *moleskin* at a backpacking shop or a drugstore. You should always keep this peel-and-stick padding handy to take care of blisters as they start to develop. Duct tape also works for keeping "hot spots" from turning into blisters.

Clothes

These days, the clothes that are right for the backcountry—pile jackets, sports sandals, and even hiking boots—are also popular at school. But at school, many people choose their clothes based on what other people wear. For hiking and camping you need to pick your clothing based on how it performs. Does it keep you warm when it's wet? Will it dry out easily?

There are so many brands and styles of clothes that they are difficult to consider. How well an item protects you outdoors will depend greatly on the material it's made of—even the best cotton shirt won't keep you warm when it's wet. To better understand the choices available, let's look at the materials.

Cotton

Clothes made of 100-percent cotton are notoriously bad for hiking, camping, canoeing, and other outdoor activities. They're cold when wet and slow to dry out. All-cotton T-shirts, pants (blue jeans), sweaters, socks, and long johns can also be found in blends that will dry faster and keep you warmer. A blend of nylon and cotton makes for lightweight pants or shorts that will outperform pure cotton by a wide margin, and T-shirts made of a 50-50 blend of cotton and synthetic are better for outdoor wear too.

Wool

Nothing beats wool in the winter. A wool sweater keeps you warm on the wettest of days, but because wool is slow to dry and can be itchy next to your skin you should layer it over other clothes. In socks, a wool-polypropylene or other wool-synthetic blend will keep your feet comfortable on a long hike.

the all-wool approach

Nylon

This synthetic is cheap to buy, quick to dry, and resistant to abrasion. There are dozens of varieties of nylon, including rugged Cordura and soft Supplex. Alone and in blends, nylon is a multipurpose fiber that will find its way into everything from your boots and socks to your sleeping bag and pack.

Silk

Silk is a strong, lightweight fabric that makes an excellent first layer, giving warmth without bulk for clothes such as long johns. It dries slowly but it insulates well even when wet. The downside to silk is that it tends to wear out at the seams more quickly than synthetics do. It also must be hand washed and line dried.

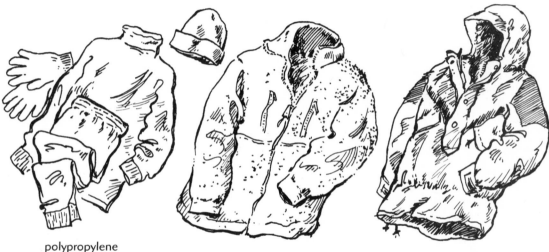

polypropylene
hat, gloves, and underwear

pile jacket

nylon windbreaker

Polypropylene and Polyesters

These lightweight petroleum-based materials are often used in socks and long johns. They keep you warm when wet and they dry out quickly because they wick away moisture instead of soaking it in. The problems with polypro are that it retains odors particularly well and it must be line dried because it will shrink and melt in the dryer. Polyester is a hollow-core fabric that traps air in its fibers to provide extra insulation. It can be machine washed and dried and doesn't retain odors.

Pile

Synthetic pile or fleece, like Polartec, makes comfortable jackets and pants that layer well with other clothes. It dries quickly and offers superior warmth and comfort even when wet. Pile clothes are bulky and too warm to hike in, but lightweight to carry.

Layering

You need your clothing to be flexible when you spend a lot of time outdoors. You'll start out cold in the morning, heat up us the sun gets high overhead, and find yourself cooling off again at night. Layering your clothes will help you adapt to these fluctuations and respond to changes in the weather.

Layering is particularly important in cold weather. You should remember that your clothes don't *give* you warmth but *trap in* your own body heat.

A good layering system for cold weather combines long johns made of silk or a synthetic, pants (wool or pile) and a shirt, an insulated parka, a parka shell, mittens over liner gloves, a balaclava (knit hood and face shield), and a hat. If no snow is expected, a wool sweater can substitute for the parka. The shell gear will protect you from wind as well as rain. Take off a layer as you heat up, and add a layer when the temperature drops.

In mild weather your layering system doesn't need to be so cumbersome. On a cool fall or spring morning, shorts and a T-shirt topped with a pile jacket and pile pants will probably be enough to keep you warm when you start out. As you warm up you can take off first the pants and then the jacket to keep from overheating.

a mild weather t-shirt can be topped with pile jacket and pile pants

polymer t-neck

Gore-Tex windbreaker or pile jacket

vapor barrier shirt

polymer liner sock

vapor barrier sock

heavy wool sock

Rain Gear

Of you're in the outdoors often, you know that it isn't a question of whether it will rain, but when and for how long. Rainy camping trips can actually be fun if you're properly equipped. You have two options in rain gear: ponchos and rainsuits. Ponchos are cheap, lightweight, and compact. The problem is that they only keep you somewhat dry in the best of conditions—in the wind they're practically useless. Most outdoor enthusiasts opt instead for a rain jacket and rain pants, which can be purchased separately or as a set.

A good rain jacket should have a hood that extends slightly in front of your face, giving you enough room to wear a knit cap or balaclava underneath. Adjustable cuffs will let you tighten them over gloves in cold weather or let in air in hot weather. The fewer the seams any rain gear has, the better, because this is where water first works its way in. The zipper can also let water into your coat unless it's covered by a snap-down storm flap. A drawstring bottom pulls tight to keep you toasty in cold weather or lets you hang loose in a warm rain.

billed hood

Velcro cuffs

underarm zipper

zippered inside and snap or Velcro closures

sealed pockets

storm flap

Waterproof-Breathables vs. Coated

A jacket made with a laminate, such as Gore-Tex, uses a thin, lightweight membrane between the outer shell and the inner liner of the coat. This membrane, made of a form of Teflon, has nine billion microscopic holes per inch that create a waterproof yet breathable fabric. The holes are big enough to let water vapor out, but far too small to let liquid in.

The problem with waterproof-breathable material is that dirt and oil clog the tiny holes and cut down on the fabric's efficiency. You can bring back off-the-rack performance by washing the jacket with a nondetergent soap and machine drying it. The factory-sealed seams must be repaired at the factory or an authorized service center. Garments made with breathable-waterproof laminates are often twice as expensive as those made with coated nylon.

Coated nylon rainsuits keep you dry but they don't breathe to keep you cool, which means you'll sweat more and get wet from the inside instead of from the rain. Nylon rain gear is fine to wear around camp when you won't be exerting yourself, but it can heat you up quickly on the trail. The seams must be sealed just like tent seams to be effective. Coated nylon gear is inexpensive and comes in a variety of styles.

Gaiters

In addition to a rain jacket and pants you may want to carry a pair of gaiters. Usually made of a tough coated nylon, gaiters wrap around the bottom of your rain pants and the top of your boots to keep water and snow from working down into the boots. Gaiters keep boots dryer and make them last longer, and they'll also keep out sticks, rocks, and other bits of trail trash.

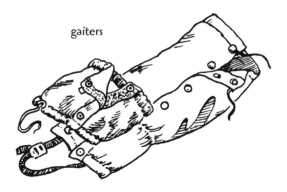

gaiters

Backpacks

A backpack is your passport to simplicity. It can carry everything you need to live as you travel through rarely visited back-country areas. Finding the right pack starts with deciding between the two basic frame choices: external or internal. Each style has its own strengths and weaknesses to consider.

External-Frame Packs

The external-frame pack is easy to identify by its visible metal or plastic support rods. This pack has a high center of gravity—a good feature if you are carrying a heavy load of 50 pounds or more, but liable to throw you off balance when you're bushwhacking through rough terrain or hopping from rock to rock on a rugged trail. For this reason, the external-frame pack is the best choice for carrying heavy loads on well-established trails. It also costs much less than a comparable internal-frame pack.

It's easier to organize your gear in an external-frame pack because it often has numerous exterior pockets, a top-loading upper compartment, and a front-panel-loading lower compartment. You can usually strap your sleeping bag onto the frame beneath the pack and your sleeping pad or tent on top.

Pack manufacturers list the number of cubic inches their pack will carry so you can compare pack volumes. An external-frame pack of about 3,000 cubic inches is a good size for most backpacking trips. Most external-frame packs come with an expandable top compartment that can add about 1,000 cubic inches for bulky gear or long hikes.

The external-frame pack has a suspended backband that holds it away from your back. This adds ventilation and makes the pack more comfortable on hot-weather hikes than the form-fitting internal-frame pack. When you try on external-frame packs, the fit of the waist belt is most important. The well-padded hip belt should carry most of the weight of the pack.

The pack is connected to the frame with *clevis pins* and *split rings* or straps. The rings can work loose or break as you hike, so you should carry a spare in your repair kit. It's easier to use real pins and rings to fix your pack on the trail than to improvise.

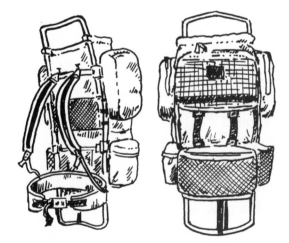

Internal-Frame Packs

Flexible stays made of composite, graphite, or aluminum form the hidden frame in an internal-frame pack. This pack has a low center of gravity and fits every contour of your body to make mountaineering and rockhopping easier.

A thin sheet of flexible plastic is sewn into the pack to keep gear from poking into your back, but you need to pack an internal-frame pack carefully to make sure it's comfortable to wear. The gear must be strapped in tight to help form the pack support system, and everything you carry should fit inside. You can strap only lightweight gear (such as a sleeping pad or an ice axe) to the outside.

Most internal-frame packs have no pockets except for optional add-on pockets made by the manufacturer. There is usually one top-loading compartment, in addition to the sleeping bag compartment in the bottom of the pack. Because this pack is arranged like a duffel bag, it's important to develop a good system for packing. Use stuff sacks for organizing so you don't have to fish around in your pack to find the gear you need.

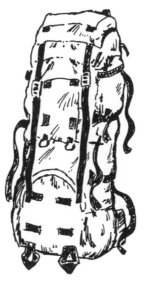

In spite of these minor drawbacks, internal-frame packs have become the favorite of many backpackers for the body-hugging way they carry loads on rugged trails. Because the sleeping bag is carried inside the pack, you need about 1,000 more cubic inches than in an external-frame pack. An internal-frame pack with a capacity of 4,000 cubic inches is the right size for most hikers.

Features to Look for in External-Frame Packs

A cleanly welded, tubular aluminum frame

Coated nylon packcloth to offer water resistance

Even stitching with reinforcement at stress points

Padded shoulder straps

A mesh backband to allow extra ventilation in hot weather

Plenty of room between your head and the pack frame

Exterior pockets for easy organization

A thick foam hipbelt with a quick-release buckle

Features to Look for in Internal-Frame Packs

Contoured composite, graphite, or aluminum stays

Compression straps to cinch smaller loads tight

Padded shoulder straps and hip belt

A sternum strap to hold the pack close to your chest

Even stitching with reinforcement at stress points

A lumbar pad, which fits into the small of your back to comfortably distribute the load and improve ventilation

Cinch straps at the waist and shoulder to fit the load to your pack

Lash points to carry gear outside the pack

A slim profile with add-on pockets

A reinforced pack bottom

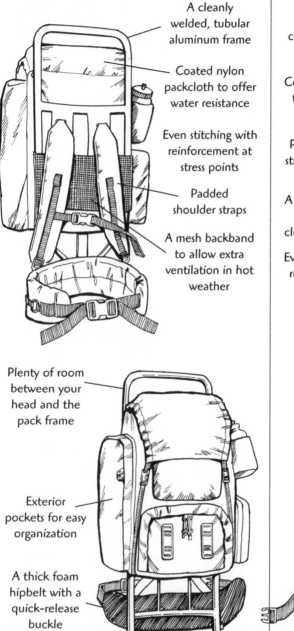

Pack Covers

Even the best packs are only water resistant, not waterproof, making pack covers a necessary piece of equipment. You can buy a poncho-style cover that fits over both you and the pack, but this is easily blown about in the wind so that you both get wet anyway. Separate rain gear for you and the pack is your best bet.

The pack cover should fit all the way around the pack, with cinch straps or elastic to hold it in place so that it can't easily be blown or pulled loose. Seal all the seams on the pack cover as you would for a tent. Pack it in an external pocket or other easy-to-reach spot. If your pack will have to stay outside the tent at night, carry a big garbage bag to wrap up the pack and cover in case of rain or dew.

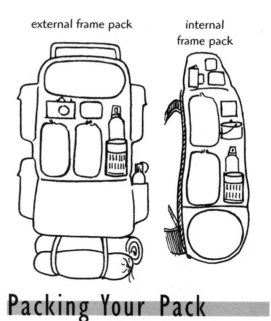

external frame pack   internal frame pack

How Much to Carry

A rule of thumb is to never carry more than a third of your body weight, but you'll be even more comfortable if you can get your pack weight down to a quarter of your weight. If your pack weighs 50 pounds, and you weigh only 100 or so, it's time to take a hard look at your gear. Trim the weight to a manageable amount.

sleeping bag
toilet kit
water purifier
pots
food
rain gear
foam pad
flashlight
first aid kit
repair kit
nylon cord
stove
canteen
tent
clothes

Packing Your Pack

For hiking on well-established trails, carry the heaviest gear at the top of the pack to center the weight over your body. For off-trail hiking or on rugged trails, keep the heavy gear in the bottom of the pack to lower your center of gravity and improve your balance. Girls have a naturally lower center of gravity and often find it more comfortable to pack the heavy items toward the bottom of the pack no matter what the trail is like.

For any terrain the weight should be distributed evenly from side to side. Cook kits and tent stakes can poke you in the back, so pack hard or sharp gear away from you and use clothing and other soft items for padding.

There are some items, such as rain gear, a water bottle, and perhaps a camera, that you'll want to have quick access to. Pack them in easy-to-reach spots such as side pockets or at the top of the pack. Strap the camera on your waist belt or sternum strap to keep it close at hand.

Color-coded stuff sacks are a great way to organize your pack. Finding your toothbrush, for example, might be tricky unless you know that your toiletries are always in the green sack. If you stick to the same system of packing on trip after trip, finding your gear will become second nature.

Putting On Your Pack

On a backpacking trip you will be putting your pack on and taking it off several times a day. There are two ways to put on or take off a pack. The first is to have a second hiker assist you by picking up your pack and holding it steady while you slip into the shoulder straps and fasten the hip belt. The other hiker can also give one last look at your pack to make sure it seems to be packed tight. This is the easiest method, but you won't always have a second hiker around.

Another way to pull on a pack is to set it up on one knee with the shoulder straps facing you. Pull the pack onto one shoulder and then the other. Tighten the hip belt and you're ready to go.

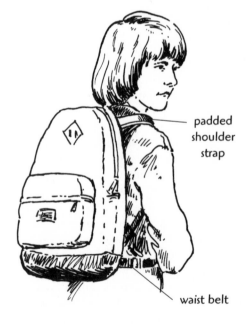

padded shoulder strap

waist belt

Daypacks

Cheap daypacks are everywhere, used as bookbags and even purses, but they aren't all strong enough for many days on the trail. Look for a double-bottomed pack with heavy reinforced stitching. The back of the pack should be padded to keep hard objects from poking you, and the shoulder straps should be padded as well. The waist belt is just for keeping the bag from swinging around on your back and doesn't need to be padded like the one on your backpack. Pockets for smaller items, such as a map and a compass, will help you organize the pack better.

Repair Kits

Resourcefulness is essential in the back-country. Part of taking care of yourself in a roadless wilderness is the ability to repair your gear in the field. Stack the deck in your favor by carrying a repair kit with the items you need to fix your stove, tent, pack, and other equipment.

Camp stoves are the equipment that need the most attention, but if you read and follow the manufacturer's directions for using your stove you'll avoid many problems that call for repairs. Most stove manufacturers sell a kit with replacement parts and instructions for using them.

You can buy a tent repair kit in a back-packing store that will work for your pack cover and other waterproof materials as well. A good kit will include fabric tape, a short length of cord, a mosquito netting patch, and a needle and thread.

Round out your repair kit with some multi-colored threads and a tiny pair of scissors, which you can find in the inexpensive travelers' sewing kits sold in grocery and drug stores.

One last item to keep handy is duct tape. A little duct tape can fix a lot of problems: patching a rip in a sleeping bag, covering a hot spot that's threatening to turn into a blister, or splinting a broken tent pole.

Toiletries

Among the toiletries campers carry are a towel, soap and/or shampoo, a toothbrush and toothpaste, toilet paper, comb, and pocket mirror. All but the towel and the toilet paper can be packed together in a stuff sack to make them easy to find in your pack.

Towel

A hand towel for drying your face and hands is all you'll need for an overnight trip. For a trip to a developed campground with showers you'll want to pack a full-size towel. You may want to consider buying a towel made especially for backpacking. They're lightweight, super-absorbent, and quick-drying so you don't have to carry the weight of a water-soaked towel.

All-Purpose Soap

There are several biodegradable soaps available for campers. Though these soaps decompose more easily than soaps and shampoos made for home use, they are not to be used in streams or lakes or within 200 feet of a water source. Even if it's not a water source for your campsite, it's a source of water for numerous plants and animals. Whatever soap you choose, use it sparingly.

Toothbrush and Toothpaste

You can use a plastic toothbrush holder to bring your toothbrush from home, or you can try a lightweight traveler's toothbrush that fits inside its own hollow plastic handle when not in use.

Baking soda (carried in double plastic bags) makes an earth-friendly toothpaste. Whatever toothpaste you use, you should brush your teeth in the bathhouse at a developed campground. In the backcountry, walk well away from camp and rinse using only treated water. Even the small amount of water used for rinsing your teeth is enough for you to get giardiasis and other bacteria from untreated water. Dental floss cleans between teeth and works well in cold weather.

Toilet Paper

One roll of unscented white toilet paper in a resealable plastic bag should be enough for two campers to share. To cut down on bulk, squeeze the center cardboard tube flat. For shorter trips you can pack a partially used roll from home. Toilet paper should be packed out of sensitive areas where no facilities are provided.

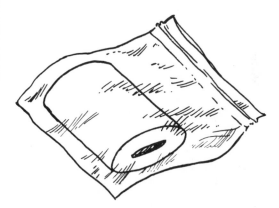

Other Toiletries

Other items that may go in your toiletries bag include cleaning fluid and other contact lens supplies, sunscreen, prescription medication, pain reliever, and vitamins. This is where girls will want to pack feminine hygiene products, along with a plastic bag for packing out.

Deodorant is a nonessential item that makes its way into many campers' packs. It's best left at home, but if you must bring it, buy a sample size of unscented deodorant.

Lighting

After the sun sets, with no campfire to illuminate the camp, everyone may turn in earlier than they want to, especially on short winter nights. You'll want to carry at least a flashlight or a candle and you may consider carrying a lantern as well.

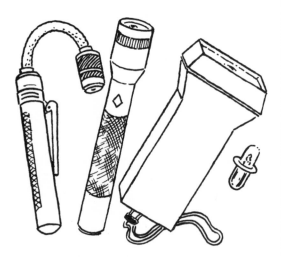

Flashlights

A small flashlight powered by two AA batteries will provide enough light to get you around camp after dark. Flashlights powered by D batteries are bulky and heavy, and they provide more light than you'll need. Make sure your batteries are fresh, or carry some extras. Even if you take a lantern you'll want a flashlight too, for instance when nature calls after dark. You can buy a headband for a penlight-shaped flashlight so you can use it hands-free like a headlight.

Headlights

Head-mounted illumination comes in handy for nighttime chores around camp. With your headlight on, you have light everywhere you look. Some lamps hold the batteries on the headband and others use a remote battery pack that attaches to your belt or pack. A one-piece unit should be lightweight to prevent headaches when you wear it for long periods.

Two-piece headlights have wires running from the headlight to the battery pack. These wires can get tangled easily, so if you plan to wear the headlight for a while you may want to run the wires inside your shirt to keep them out of the way.

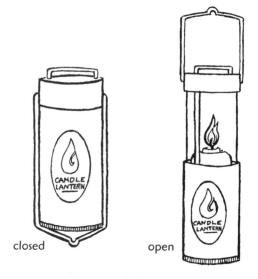

closed   open

candle lantern

Lanterns

Camping lanterns come in a variety of sizes and may burn butane, propane, white gas, or a candle. With the exception of the dim candle lantern, they can all be adjusted for brightness. This is important in developed campgrounds, where you'll need to dim your lantern as your neighbors turn in for the night.

The small candle lantern gives out just enough light for one camper to cook, clean up, or read by. It's much safer than a candle alone because it's housed in a metal and glass container that cuts back on the fire hazard of an open flame.

Small fuel lanterns provide enough light for most campers, even in large groups. There are several models that fit on a butane or propane fuel bottle. The butane lantern is lightweight enough for backpacking and you can use your butane stove's fuel bottle rather than carrying a separate fuel cartridge. The propane lantern, as well as the small white gas lanterns that are also available, are too heavy to carry in a pack.

Full-size camp lanterns are fueled by white gas or propane from a bulk tank. These powerhouses give off lots of light when they're turned up full blast.

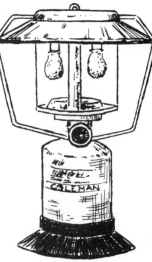

Coleman
propane
lantern

Peak 1 lantern

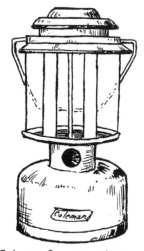

Coleman fluorescent lantern

Knives

A folding knife has many uses around camp and can double as a dinner knife for weight-conscious backpackers. The best choice for camping is a multifeature Swiss Army–style knife with a single 3-inch or 4-inch blade. The extra features, such as an awl, a screwdriver, and a can opener, save the blade for fine cutting and can lengthen its useful life. The long blade of a sheath knife looks good, but it's harder to carry and gives you no advantage over a folding knife for camp chores.

Take good care of your knife by wiping the blade after each use and keeping the whole knife as clean and dry as possible. Oil the joints occasionally with household or cooking oil. Never put the blade in a flame because the intense heat will soften the edge of the blade.

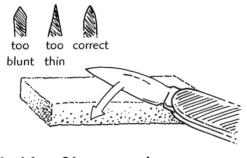

too blunt   too thin   correct

Knife Sharpening

Sharpening your knife removes nicks and gives the blade a sharp, smooth edge. Begin with an oiled coarse sharpening stone to take off any rough spots on the edge of the blade. When the blade is smooth, switch to a dry smooth stone. Lay the blade with its sharp edge against the stone and the dull edge angled up slightly toward you. Pull the knife over the stone from the base to the point of the blade in one smooth stroke. Repeat the motion three more times. Flip the knife over and give the other side four pulls across the stone. Continue switching sides until the knife is sharp.

Don't overdo it: an oversharpened knife has a fine edge that quickly dulls. When the blade can slice neatly through a sheet of paper, it's sharp enough to use. If you do oversharpen it, rub, or *strop*, each side of the blade backward over a piece of leather several times to wear it down.

Even new knives must be sharpened. They come with a machine edge that needs honing before it's put to work.

Hatchets

Once considered a necessity for any camper, axes and hatchets are now left at home by many outdoor enthusiasts who wish to leave no trace of their visit. There are times, however, when you may need a hatchet to cut up dead and downed wood.

Using a Hatchet

Always cut with a chopping block to keep the blade from digging into the ground. To chop branches up to 3 inches thick, place the blade across the branch and keep it poised there as you lift them together about a foot and a half off the block. Bring them both down to hit the chopping block in one swift, smooth motion. This method can also be used to split small wood in two if you lay the blade lengthwise along the log.

For thicker wood, lay the branch on a chopping block and alternate the angle of your strokes to cut a V notch into the wood. After making several angled cuts from each direction, make one straight cut into the notch to clear it. Repeat the angled cuts until the notch breaks through the other side.

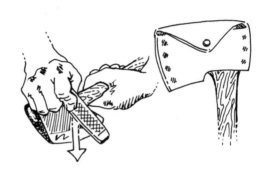

Caring for a Hatchet

Like a knife, a hatchet or axe needs to be kept clean and sharp to cut effectively. Keep the blade sheathed when it's not in use.

Use a flat file to smooth nicks off the blade and sharpen the edge. Hold the blade flat in one hand. With the other hand, file from bottom to top of the cutting edge, pushing the file away from you over the blade. Turn the blade over and file from top to bottom.

Occasionally you'll want to use a dry stone to return a sharp edge to the blade. Work from the bottom edge of the blade to the top, rubbing the stone against the blade in a circular motion. Turn the blade around and work the other side from top to bottom with the same circular motion. Repeat until the blade is sharp.

After sharpening the blade with either a file or a dry stone, finish by stropping it with leather or a smooth piece of wood to dull the fine edge for chopping.

Selecting a Campsite

Whether you're camping in your backyard or in a wilderness area 20 miles from the nearest road, it's important to select a good campsite. So, what *is* a good campsite? You need good water, room to camp, and the right terrain. Your campsite should be able to withstand the impact of your stay for the night. That means that large groups should stay in established campsites, and even two people must be careful not to camp in fragile areas.

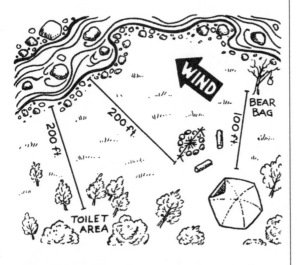

Water

A good campsite must have a reliable source of water nearby. In a campground that water source will be a water faucet. On the trail it may be a spring or a stream, and unless you're planning to carry all your water along with you, you'll need to purify the water you drink.

Room for Tents

The second most important criterion for a good campsite is enough open area to pitch your tent or tents without being too exposed. Remember, if you're in a mountain meadow during a thunderstorm, a lightning bolt will find your tent an attractive target. Trees around your campsite will protect you from the wind but they may drip on you long after the rain has stopped. The ideal site is a fairly level area in a small clearing in the woods. Another good site is at the edge of a meadow with high trees nearby. Though it may be picturesque, a site on the banks of a stream is a bad idea. A basic minimum-impact camping concept is to set up camp at least 200 feet away from any water source. Camping near streams can also be dangerous in areas (such as southwestern canyons) that are prone to flash floods.

Slightly Sloping Terrain

Pick a site that is flat or on a very slight slope. Don't pick a low spot because rain will puddle up around or under your tent. If the slope is more than very slight, you'll spend the night slowly sliding down the tent and waking up to crawl back into position again. Pitch your tent with its entrance downslope and sleep with your head at the high end. You can test drive a tent-site by lying down on the ground to find the most comfortable position before you pitch the tent.

Designated Sites

Sometimes you won't have a choice of camp-site. Many campgrounds will assign you a site when you check in, but these designated sites are almost always just right. If the site you're assigned has too little or even too much room, you may suggest to the person who assigned it that another would be better for your group. Want to get to sleep early? Your best bet is a campsite away from the bath houses and the main road.

No Room in the Backcountry?

The busiest National Park backcountry is in Virginia's Shenandoah National Park. This park logs one overnight stay in the backcountry each year for every five acres of park. The least populated is Yellowstone, with only one backcountry night per 50 acres.

Making Camp

Before you lay out the groundcloth for your tent, get down on your hands and knees and remove all the sticks and rocks from the tent site. If there are roots sticking out of the ground, look for another spot. Ever wonder how the fairy tale princess could feel a pea through dozens of mattresses? Sleep on a small rock or root and find out! Preparing a relatively smooth spot now will make for a much better night's sleep later on.

Lay out your groundcloth and try out your tent site. This is the best way to feel for lurking rocks and roots and to tell if your site is on too steep a slope. Pitch your tent and roll out your sleeping pad and sleeping bag first thing. That way you won't have to fumble around in the dark later on to get settled for the night. It will also give your sleeping bag time to return to its maximum loft so it'll keep you warmer.

In heavy winds, set up your tent with its entrance sheltered away from the wind. An A-frame tent should be in line with the wind so its sides don't bear the force of the wind.

If you're car camping, lock any unused gear in the car to discourage theft. Keep your personal gear with you inside the tent if there's room. If you're backpacking, hang your pack from a nearby tree with the top of the pack at eye level so it's safe but accessible. Cover it with a big trash bag at night to keep out the rain or dew. Don't keep your food and other smellables in the pack when you hang it up for the night.

Backcountry "Bathrooms"

Another important part of setting up camp for the night is selecting a site for your "bathroom." If you're staying in a developed campground, there will probably be toilets nearby. You must use these to reduce your impact on a heavily used area. If a toilet is not available you will have to improvise. When you set up camp the group should decide on the best area for the bathroom. Remember that it needs to be 200 feet from any stream, spring, or other water source, and well out of sight of the camp and trail.

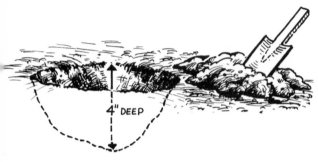

Always dig a "cat hole" to bury your waste. Use your backpacker's trowel to cover the waste with at least 4 inches of dirt. This advice is time tested, to say the least. In Deuteronomy 23:13, Moses wrote, "designate a place outside the camp where you can go to relieve yourself . . . dig a hole and cover up your excrement." This 3,500-year-old decree is still the best way to handle waste in camp. The only new advice is to carry out your toilet paper.

A group of four or more camping more than one night in the same location needs to improvise a privy. Use a camp shovel (a backpacker's trowel is too small for this task) to dig a pit about 1 foot deep, 2 feet long, and 6 inches wide. Leave the shovel by the pile of displaced dirt next to the hole, with a roll of unscented toilet paper in a plastic bag. After you use the pit, "flush" by covering your waste with a heavy sprinkling of dirt from the pile. When you break camp, completely fill in the

hole and recover the area with forest litter to disguise the filled-in trench. This technique causes some long-term problems for a campsite because such a large amount of feces decomposes very slowly. This is just one reason why large groups should always stay in established camping areas. In a sensitive area, such as an alpine meadow, leave-no-trace guidelines call for groups to carry out all their waste in an ammo can or Tupperware container.

If it is winter and snowing, dig into the ground beneath the snow or you will leave an unpleasant surprise for campers to discover in springtime. If the ground is frozen too hard to cut into with a camper's trowel, pack out your waste. It sounds horrifying, but it's easy. Just line a hole in the snow with a plastic bag. Do your thing, seal the bag, and pack it out.

Pack It Out

Human waste decomposes slowly when buried and leaves an unsightly, smelly mess when left out to rot. To *really* leave no trace you have to pack it out in a resealable plastic container (such as Tupperware) or an old ammo can. Dispose of your waste at home. This may sound extreme, but some backcountry areas don't have any good sites for burying waste.

Whether or not you pack out your waste, you should pack out your toilet paper. It takes a long time to decompose and it creates an area that looks like a cotton patch if it's not buried deep enough.

Setting up the Kitchen

Hanging up a bag of smellables is just one way to keep your encounters with bears from being too close for comfort. Your kitchen area will create smells that a curious bear will find irresistible. If you set up your kitchen well away from your tent you'll keep the bear from foraging in the tent for dinner.

Campfire Rings

If you plan to have a campfire, use the ring provided at your campsite. When a campfire ring is not provided, check to see if fires are allowed. To build a campfire ring, clean out leaves and other debris from an area about 3 feet across. Find large stones to form the ring around the fire. Make sure you place the stones on the bare ground, not on leaves, or the leaves will smolder up under the hot rocks and the fire will spread beyond the ring.

Don't get the stones for your campfire ring from a stream or its banks. Rocks that sit under water for long periods of time absorb water into their cracks. Heat turns the water to steam and causes the rock to explode, sending shards in every direction. We've had a hole ripped through our tent by a piece of rock that had just zinged past our heads, and we speak from experience when we say this is a sight you don't want to see!

After you've made the campfire ring, and before you build the fire, fill a canteen and set it nearby to contain the fire if it spreads.

Change Shoes in Camp

Hiking boots help your feet grip the trail, but they can tear up campsites. Change to lightweight shoes, such as river sandals, tennis shoes, or water socks to keep from tearing up the soil around camp.

"But all conservation of wilderness is self-defeating, for to cherish we must see and fondle, and when enough have seen and fondled, there is no wilderness left to cherish."

—Aldo Leopold,
A Sand County
Almanac

Building a Campfire

ampfires are closely linked to many people's idea of camping. They are also the most visible sign that a camper has ignored the leave-no-trace ideal. No matter how careful you are, a campfire will leave its mark on your campsite. If you must build a fire, do so in an established campsite and bring your own wood for all but the smallest fire. Of course, if it is an emergency (such as to prevent hypothermia when a stove is unavailable or not working), you'll have to build a fire to keep warm.

When you gather firewood, select only downed, dead wood from a wide area. It's irresponsible to cut up a live tree for your fire, and green wood won't burn well anyway. Be sure to get plenty of twigs (about as thick as a matchstick) for kindling. You will need to add progressively larger pieces of wood as the fire starts burning in earnest.

Fires need both fuel and oxygen to burn. The most common calamity faced by firebuilders is for a fire to light, take hold, and quickly burn out its supporting wood, causing the fuel to fall in on the flames and choke out the fire. No matter how much wood you use, the fire will die without air to breathe.

The fires shown here are designed to keep the air flowing while you add fuel.

Tepee Fire

This fire is built from a cone of small branches shaped like an Indian tepee. Start by planting an inch-thick piece of wood into the dirt or ashes in your fire pit, deep enough for it to support itself. Lean smaller sticks around this central pole to form three-quarters of a tepee, leaving open the side away from the wind so that you can light the fire and add wood.

Break up your small twigs for kindling. If you have a fire starter, place it inside the tepee and pile the twigs around and over it. If you don't have a fire starter, mix a few dried leaves in with the twigs. Light the fire starter or leaves; the fire should get going easily. As it burns, continue to feed it by leaning more wood against the tepee, always making sure that you don't pile on too much wood at once and smother the fire.

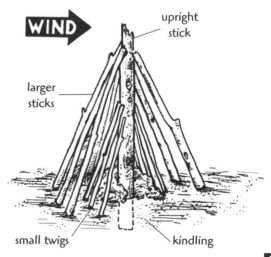

WIND

upright stick

larger sticks

small twigs

kindling

storyteller's fire

lean-to fire

log cabin
fire

cooking over a
lean-to fire

Log Cabin Fire

This fire starts with a tepee fire. When the tepee has burned down to hot coals and low flames, lay two large (3- to 4-inch-thick) pieces of wood parallel to each other on opposite sides of the fire. The logs should be touching the coals of the tepee fire.

Lay two more logs across the first two to form a square. Continue adding progressively smaller logs as you build up the sides of the log cabin. Six to eight layers of logs should be enough to give your fire plenty of big fuel to burn. The log cabin spacing gives air room to circulate.

Storyteller's Fire

When you're telling stories or doing skits by the campfire, you don't want to be constantly poking and fueling the fire. The storyteller's fire burns for a long time without extra fuel or care. This is a large fire that is not for use in the backcountry.

Begin with two 4-inch-thick logs placed about 2½ feet apart inside the fire ring. Lay six slightly smaller logs across the first two, leaving a couple of inches between each log. Continue layering with progressively thinner and shorter pieces of wood to build a pyramid shape.

By the time the pyramid is about 2½ feet

tall you should be using kindling-size wood. Place your fire starter (or dry leaves and twigs) on top of this layer of small sticks and light it. When the top layer is burning well, leave the fire alone. It will burn down through the stack of wood, feeding on progressively larger logs.

Lean-to Fire

Start with one log at least 4 inches thick. If you can't find any dead, downed wood this big, use a large rock instead. (Don't take one of the rocks out of the fire ring—find another.) Put this base log or rock inside the fire pit and set the fire starter up against it. Arrange kindling around and over the fire starter, leaving room for air to circulate. Lean pieces of wood against the base to form a "shed roof" over the kindling. Light the fire starter. As the kindling begins to burn through the wood of the lean-to, continue to lean more sticks against the base to feed the fire.

The lean-to fire isn't suited to large campfires but it's a good choice if you're forced to cook over a fire. When the fire has burned down to hot coals you can lay a second log or rock parallel to the first and close enough to balance a cooking pot between them. Make sure your pot is steady on the rocks before you let go of it.

Putting Out the Fire

Even when a fire has burned out completely there will still be hot coals in the ashes. You must take extra steps to make the fire pit safe for the night or when you break camp.

Pour water from a canteen into your hand and dribble it through your fingers onto the ashes.

Stir the coals with a stick and sprinkle again. Continue until no steam rises up from the coals.

Before you leave the fire pit, feel the ashes with your hands to make sure they're cold.

Make a fire-starter and waterproof matches

For this project you will need:

    a pot for boiling water on a kitchen stove
    a tin can with its label stripped off
    paraffin wax or a candle string
    a piece of cardboard at least 6 inches by 6 inches
    a dozen wooden kitchen matches

1. Cut the paraffin or candle into small pieces (about 1 inch square) and place them in the tin can.
2. Bring a pot of water to a boil on the stove, set the can into the boiling water, and allow the wax to melt.
3. While the wax is melting, tear or cut the cardboard into strips (about a half-dozen strips is plenty) about 1 inch wide and 5 inches long. Roll up the strips and tie each one with string, leaving a 6-inch tail.
4. When the wax is melted, turn off the stove and move the pot to another burner. Hold a cardboard roll by its string and dip it into the hot wax. Pull it out when it's soaked and let the excess wax drip back into the tin can. Set the roll to dry on a piece of unused cardboard.
5. After dipping all the cardboard rolls, dip the striking ends of the matches into the hot wax and set them aside to dry. When the wax has cooled, throw away the tin can, pour out the water, and put the pot away. The matches are now waterproof and the wax-soaked cardboard rolls are ready to use as fire starters on your next camping trip.

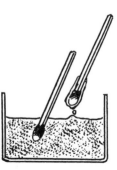

Camp Games

After camp is set up and before you crash for the night, there's usually time and energy left over for a few games. These games are for small groups—a pair of campers can just play cards and swap lies.

Assassin

Five or more players

The group sits in a circle facing each other. All the players but one close their eyes and bow their heads. The remaining player walks around the circle and picks the assassin by tapping one person lightly on top of the head, then leaves the circle and says, "Ready."

The other players look around and make eye contact with everyone else in the circle. The assassin "kills" other players by winking at them. The player killed should wait at least 15 seconds and make eye contact with several other players before announcing, "I'm dead." The assassin must be careful not to let the others catch him winking. If a player thinks she knows who the assassin is she says, "I have an accusation." If another player thinks he also knows who the assassin is, he says, "I'll back you up." At the count of three, they say the name of their suspect together. If they agree and are correct, the assassin loses and must sit out the next game by choosing the next assassin. If they are wrong, the game continues until all but the assassin and one other player are dead.

Nightstalker

Three or more players

One player sits in the middle of an open area, blindfolded and holding a flashlight. Four bandanas are placed about 10 feet out from the blindfolded player, spaced well apart. The rest of the players walk about 50 feet away to begin the game. One at a time, players try to sneak up on the blindfolded player, take a bandana, and return with it to the group. When the blindfolded player hears someone, she can point the flashlight in that player's direction and turn it on. If she hits him with the beam, he's out. The players continue taking turns until they're all out or all the bandanas have been recovered. The person with the most bandanas wins.

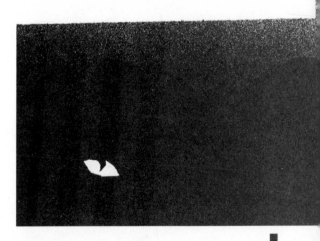

Touch and List

Four or more players

The game leader collects 10 small objects, such as a pebble, a pine needle, a leaf, a key, a pocketknife, and so on, without letting the players see what the objects are. The players sit in a row wearing blindfolds. The leader hands the first player an object and the player passes it down the line. The leader continues handing objects and the players continue passing them down the line until they've all felt all 10 objects. They take off their blindfolds and write down the 10 objects. The winner is the player who identifies the most objects. If there is a tie, the winner is the one who lists the objects closest to the order in which they were passed.

Singer's Battle

Three or more players

One player is selected to be It. That player points to another player, who must start singing a song and keep singing until It points to another player. Now that player must begin singing. If you don't start singing right away, or if you repeat a song already sung, you're out. The last player left wins and becomes It for the next round.

There are lots of variations to this game: Each player pointed to names a song and the band that plays it, or names a kind of animal, and so on. Once again, if you pause more than a few seconds when pointed to, or name something another player has already named, you're out.

Add to the Story

Two or more players

The first player begins telling a story and each player adds to the story without finishing it. Any player who can't add to the story, or who finishes it, is out. The last remaining player brings the story to a plausible ending and wins the game.

A First Aid Kit

A 6-inch-wide elastic wrap for a variety of uses, such as wrapping sprains, holding bandages in place, constricting snakebites, compressing heavy bleeding, and splinting a broken bone

Everyone agrees that you need to carry along a first aid kit when you head out for a hike or a camping trip. Unfortunately, not everyone agrees on what to put in that kit. The following list will make up a close-to-perfect first aid kit.

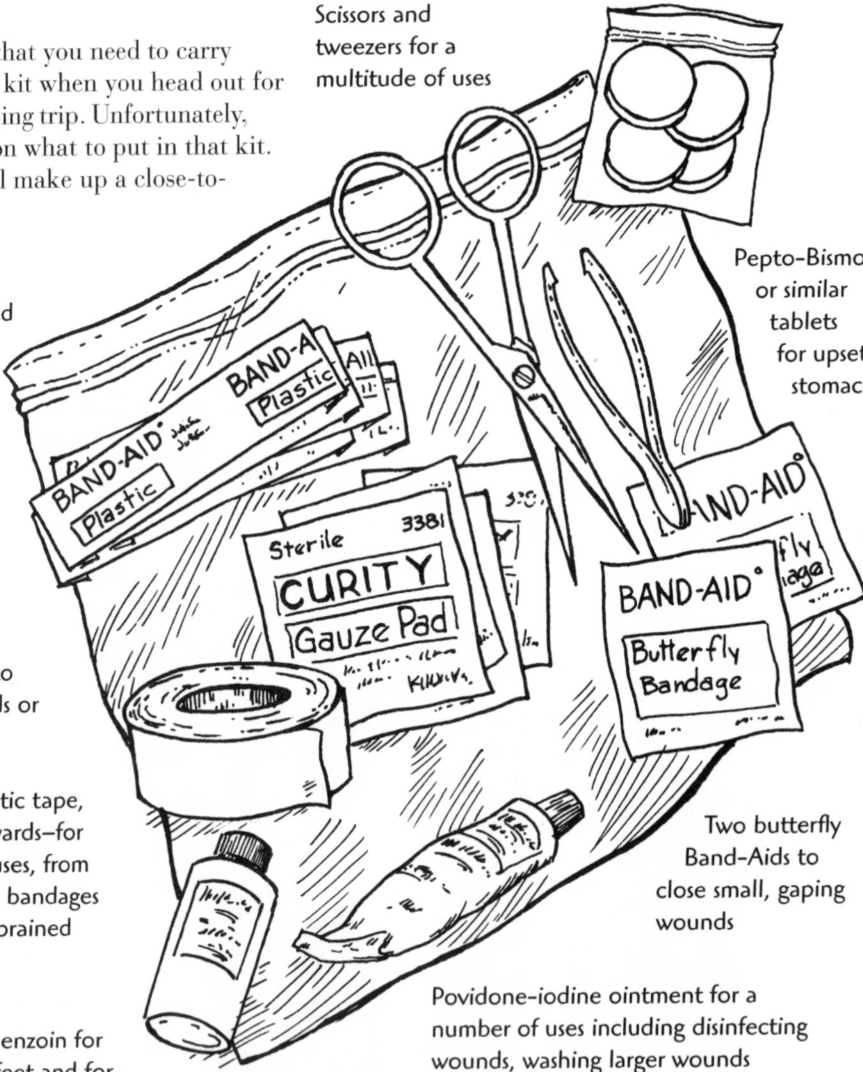

Scissors and tweezers for a multitude of uses

A zipper-lock or other waterproof bag–to hold the items in your kit

Pepto-Bismol or similar tablets for upset stomach

Approximately six 1-inch-by-3-inch Band-Aids for scratches, cuts, and scrapes

Six 4-inch-square sterile gauze pads to cover larger wounds or to stanch blood

A roll of athletic tape, 1 inch by 10 yards–for a number of uses, from holding gauze bandages to wrapping sprained ankles

Two butterfly Band-Aids to close small, gaping wounds

Tincture of benzoin for toughening feet and for rubbing on the skin to make bandages stick better

Povidone-iodine ointment for a number of uses including disinfecting wounds, washing larger wounds (when dissolved in water), and treating water in emergencies

BAND-A Plastic
BAND-AID Plastic
Sterile 3381 CURITY Gauze Pad
BAND-AID
BAND-AID Butterfly Bandage

A few antihistamine tablets for insect bites, poison ivy, and allergic reactions

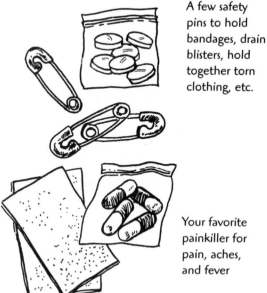

A few safety pins to hold bandages, drain blisters, hold together torn clothing, etc.

Your favorite painkiller for pain, aches, and fever

A snakebite kit (not shown)

Moleskin for hot spots and blisters

There are a number of other items you might wish to add to your first aid kit, depending on where and when you are heading outdoors. A meat tenderizer or Sting-eze will come in handy in the summer and fall when biting insects are abundant. Other possibilities are sunscreen, alcohol to help remove ticks, lip balm, skin lotion, prescription drugs (if necessary), a bee sting kit if you are allergic, and DEET repellent.

A first aid kit is very personal. Problems you have at home that require special medication will also need treatment on a camping trip. You know whether or not you suffer from constipation, for example.

Sunscreen will be an important addition to your kit if your trip will be during the summer, in the desert, or in snow. Make sure you carry a sunscreen with a sun protection factor (SPF) that matches your sensitivity to the sun. That is, if you burn easily you should carry a sunscreen with a high SPF factor, such as 30. If you are taking antibiotics, you are more sensitive to the sun's UV rays and need to block the sun with clothing as well as sunscreen.

Keep your kit as simple as possible by leaving out things you probably won't use—a suture kit, for example. Would you really sew your own or someone else's wound should the occasion arise? Repack your kit seasonally. There are some items you will need in the summer that you won't need in the winter. Always check medications for expiration dates. In an emergency, you don't want to discover that your antihistamine expired a year ago.

Before you head out on your first camping trip, whether in the backcountry or at an established group camp, it's important to be prepared for some of the medical emergencies you might meet. Your first aid kit will take care of most of the problems you'll run into but a little preparation will give you the jump on the other emergencies that could arise. Among the things to consider before you head 'em up and move 'em out are . . .

who, if anyone, in your group has existing medical problems such as allergies, diabetes, etc.

who knows what about first aid

who knows or needs to learn CPR (cardiopulmonary resuscitation), the Heimlich maneuver, artificial respiration.

At least one member of your group needs to have taken a course in basic first aid and CPR and learned how to perform artificial respiration and the Heimlich maneuver. If anyone in the group suffers from a potentially serious medical problem, you should write down everything you might need to know in an emergency, including the type of illness or allergy, the medication, where it is kept, the dosage, when it should be given, and the name and phone number of the person's doctor. Keep this information in the group first aid kit or in a designated personal first aid kit.

The following pages give a brief description of just a few of the emergencies you might encounter on a trip in the outdoors. It is by no means a comprehensive coverage of emergency first aid but it will give you some idea of what you may be up against. It cannot be said too many times that taking a course in basic first aid and CPR will give you the knowledge and confidence you need to handle a medical emergency in the outdoors.

Breathing

If a person stops breathing, he or she will die. The only way to save the life of someone who is not breathing is to perform artificial respiration. A CPR course will teach you this process. CPR has saved countless lives, particularly in near-drownings, heart attacks, and drug overdoses. For an example of just how important it is to learn CPR, try watching the TV show "Emergency 911" some evening. Don't be surprised if you see CPR used several times in one episode.

Bleeding

As you probably know, it's hard to grow up without bleeding at some point. Scraped knees and scratches are as common as milk caps (although you wouldn't want to collect them!) and they are just as easy to deal with. But what happens when you meet with a wound that needs more than a Band-Aid to stop the bleeding?

First try the usual methods, direct pressure and elevation. For example, if the cut is on the arm, raise the arm above the victim's head and press a 4-inch-square gauze pad against the wound until the bleeding stops.

What if the bleeding doesn't stop? People can and do bleed to death. Ignoring the problem won't make it go away; you need to take a basic first aid course to be able to deal with a serious wound. Call your local American Red

Cross to find out where and when they offer courses. And while you're at it, ask about a course in CPR!

Altitude Sickness

This is something you'll encounter only at altitudes greater than 8,000 feet. But as peak bagging becomes increasingly popular and mountain peaks more accessible, this serious illness, also known as Acute Mountain Sickness or AMS, becomes a real concern. Altitude sickness is serious because most people ignore their symptoms until they're in need of emergency help.

Complications from AMS almost never occur below 10,000 feet, although high altitude is officially considered to be from 8,000 to 12,000 feet. From 12,000 to 18,000 feet is considered very high and anything over that is extremely high. Your body begins to react to a change in altitude at about 4,000 feet. You may not notice it at first, but you'll begin to breathe more heavily.

How do you know if you're suffering from altitude sickness? Symptoms usually begin about 8 hours after a quick ascent and usually start with a headache, followed by a loss of appetite, nausea, listlessness, and abnormal fatigue. If you vomit and your skin looks bluish or purplish, you will soon need medical attention.

The illness has become severe when you can no longer walk in a straight line with heel touching toe. People die from AMS when fluid builds up in the lungs and brain, a condition called *edema*. It causes a crackling noise in the lungs that can be heard if someone presses an ear against your chest. Those with edema of the brain will suffer from severe headaches, hallucinations, seizures, and unconsciousness, which can be followed by coma and death.

The only way to cure this illness is to descend immediately, but it's best to prevent it in the first place. Some people can never adjust to extreme altitudes. You should get used to higher elevations gradually. Never climb from sea level to 8,000 feet in one day. Spend one night at 5,000 to 7,000 feet before ascending to 8,000 feet. Above 8,000 feet you should spend the night only 1,000 feet higher than you climbed the day before. For example, you may climb from 8,000 to 11,000 feet during the day as long as you descend back to 9,000 feet to spend the night. If you intend to go higher than 10,000 feet it would be wise to spend two whole days and nights between 8,000 and 10,000 feet before going any higher.

Mount Everest, Nepal
29,028 feet

Cerro Aconcagua, Argentina
22,831 feet

Mount McKinley, Alaska, 20,320 feet

Mount Logan, Canada, 19,850 feet

Mont Blanc, France, 15,771 feet

Mount Whitney, California, 14,494 feet

Mountains of the World

Hypothermia and Frostbite

When you're hiking in cold weather or in snow, ice, or rain, you face the dangers of frostbite and hypothermia. Humidity, wind, and wet clothing increase the effects of cold, and your body is less resistant to cold when you're tired, dehydrated, or under stress. If it's really bad outside—cold, wet, and windy—stay home. If you're already out, set up your tent and crawl into your sleeping bag. The extra warmth and rest might be all your body needs to fight the cold.

Hypothermia

Shivering, numbness, drowsiness, and extreme muscular weakness are the first signs of hypothermia. If you don't warm yourself up immediately, you'll start to experience mental confusion, impaired judgment, slurred speech, failing eyesight, and finally unconsciousness. Once you're out, it's usually not long before your heart stops beating.

When you stop shivering, you are close to death. Shivering is the body's way of keeping itself warm and if it can no longer perform this function, chances are it won't be long before other, more important, functions fail.

Remember that you're most likely to become hypothermic when you stop moving. As long as you are hiking or performing some chore that keeps you physically active, your body can keep you relatively warm. But as soon as you stop, your body's core temperature drops.

Because you can't keep moving indefinitely, you will have to keep your body warm in other ways. If it's cold and wet outside and you find yourself experiencing any of the symptoms of hypothermia, stop everything and make yourself warm. How?

If your clothes are wet, put on dry clothes if possible.

Crawl into your sleeping bag, naked if you have no dry clothes.

Make something hot to drink—tea, soup, hot chocolate (anything with a high sugar content is best; carry a packet of flavored gelatin for emergencies).

Share body heat. If someone else is hypothermic, use your body heat to warm the victim up.

If nothing seems to warm you up, then you might try building a fire for warmth. Yes, fires are a no-no in general but in this case a life is at stake.

Believe it or not, most hypothermia victims die in 40- to 50-degree weather.

Frostbite

This poetic name masks a potentially serious problem that can lead to the loss of a nose, cheeks, ears, fingers, and toes. Frostbite is caused by the formation of ice crystals on or in the fluids and soft tissues of the skin. It can become even more severe if the frostbitten area is thawed and then refrozen.

An area of skin (usually on the face, hands, or feet) that has been overexposed to the cold will begin to look flushed before turning white or grayish yellow. You may feel some pain early on but it will probably subside.

If you suspect that you have frostbite, cover the frozen area and put on extra clothing, bundle up in blankets, or double-wrap yourself in sleeping bags. If you can, go indoors; otherwise seek refuge in a tent and start warming yourself with hot liquids as you would with hypothermia.

If there is no chance that the frozen part could become refrozen, immerse it in lukewarm water (not hot!), keeping the water warm as long as possible. If water is not available, wrap the frostbitten area in blankets, clothes, or whatever else you have on hand.

You can also thaw frozen fingers in the warm confines of a partner's armpits.

Be gentle with the frostbitten area. You might be tempted to massage it to encourage the flow of blood, but you must refrain from doing so. When it thaws the area will swell, painfully, and become flushed again. When you reach this stage, stop warming the area and exercise it if possible.

Cleanse the area gently with soap and water. Rinse it and blot it dry with a clean, dry cloth. Sometimes blisters will form. Don't pop them!

Keep the affected part elevated and make sure it doesn't touch sleeping bags or blankets. If your fingers or toes have been frostbitten, put gauze between them to keep them separate. You can't walk on your toes once they've been thawed—you'll have to be carried to medical assistance, or walk with frozen toes. Don't let the frozen parts thaw if there's any chance they'll refreeze.

Until you get to help, keep the frostbitten area covered with a clean cloth. You can apply temporary bandages but make sure you keep the parts elevated and, if possible, continue to drink warm liquids.

Too Much Heat and Blistered Feet

Problems caused by heat are probably more common than those caused by cold because people are less likely to take precautions when it's hot outside. But it's easy to avoid heat-related problems. The easiest thing to do is to increase your intake of fluids. Dehydration is the leading cause of heat cramps, exhaustion, and stroke (as well as hypothermia).

When you're physically active, that is, hiking, playing sports, or working outdoors, make sure you take a break whenever the heat starts to get to you. Don't let your fear of being called a wimp push you into something *really* embarrassing. Sit down in the shade, drink some water, and let your body cool off.

Heat Cramps

Cramps are the first sign that you are heading toward heat exhaustion. The muscles of your legs and abdomen will cramp first. If you start feeling cramps, stop what you're doing immediately. Mix some salt water (one teaspoon of table salt per quart of water) and sip it at a rate of about 16 ounces over an hour. Sip, don't gulp, or you might vomit, and then you'll be worse off than you were to begin with.

According to the American National Red Cross book on first aid, you can try massaging the cramped muscles for added relief.

Heat Exhaustion

If you ignore the cramps and continue to push yourself, you'll soon experience heat exhaustion. Although your body temperature might seem normal, your skin will be pale, cool, and clammy. This could be a sign that you're about to faint–you should sit down with your head between your knees. You may also feel nauseated, sweat heavily, develop a severe headache, and become dizzy.

Once again you will need to sip salt water. You should also lie down, loosen your clothing, and raise your feet 8 to 12 inches. Apply cool, wet cloths to exposed skin. If you vomit, stop drinking the salt water. Your heat exhaustion has gone too far and you must seek medical attention.

Heat Stroke

You need to seek immediate medical attention if your heat exhaustion becomes heat stroke. How will you know if this happens? Your skin will be hot, red, and dry, and your pulse rapid and strong. You will probably become unconscious. At this point, it will no longer be up to you to diagnose your condition.

If someone in your group develops heat stroke, undress the victim and bathe the skin with cool water. If possible, place the person in a stream or other shallow body of water. Once the victim's temperature has dropped to near normal, dry him or her off. If no water is available, fan the victim with whatever you have on hand. If the body temperature rises again, start the cooling process all over again.

Heat stroke victims should never drink stimulants such as iced tea or soda that contains caffeine (Coke, Pepsi, Mountain Dew). Play it safe and use water.

Because heat stroke is a life-threatening condition, you should seek medical attention as soon as possible.

Blisters

Blisters are easier to prevent than they are to treat. As you hike, pay attention to how your feet feel. If you feel a "hot spot" on your foot, stop immediately. Take off your boot and sock and inspect your foot. If the hot spot is bright red, a blister is developing. Apply moleskin or duct tape now to keep a blister from forming. Moleskin is a padded material with self-adhesive backing made to prevent blisters. It's available in most drugstores. Cut out a piece of moleskin larger than the hot spot, peel off the paper backing, and stick it over the red area. This will stop the friction that's causing the blister.

If a blister has already formed, you don't want to pop it unless you have to. A low blister can be covered with a protective layer of moleskin or duct tape just like a hot spot, but a large blister needs to be treated if you have to keep hiking. Wash the area with soap and water. Sterilize a needle by holding it in a flame until the point turns red. As soon as the needle cools, push it into the bottom of the blister and allow the blister to drain. Apply a sterile bandage to pad the area and prevent infection.

If a blister bursts on its own, treat it like any open wound by washing it, applying an antiseptic ointment, and bandaging it.

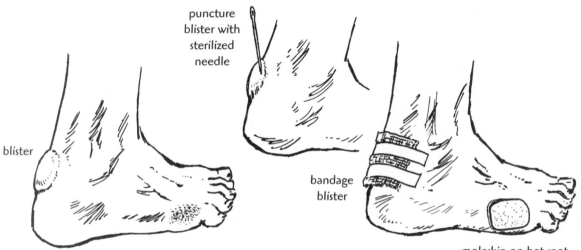

puncture blister with sterilized needle

blister

bandage blister

moleskin on hot spot

Burns

No matter how careful you are, chances are you will eventually burn yourself. It could just be the slight burn you get when you let a match burn too close to your fingers. Or it might happen if you sit too close to a campfire, light a camp stove carelessly, set your cookpot on an unsteady surface, or refuse to wear sunscreen.

First-degree burns are the most common and usually look bright red just like a bad sunburn. To treat a minor burn, immerse it in cold water or pour cold water over it. Soak a cloth in cold water and press it to the burn for 5 to 10 minutes. Allow the skin to air dry and apply aloe vera gel or antiseptic burn spray if you have it.

You can prevent sunburn by using a sunscreen with an SPF of 15 or more, but in these days of global warming, sunscreen is not the only protection you need. If you're particularly sensitive to the sun, it would be wise to avoid its rays between the hours of 10:00 A.M. and 2:00 P.M. when they're strongest. Don't trust a T-shirt for coverage—believe it or not, cotton provides an SPF of only 7 or so. If you start to feel sunburned, cover up or find shelter immediately. Continued exposure to the sun can cause severe burning and, eventually, skin cancer.

Bright red skin, blisters, and swelling are signs of a second-degree burn. Do not break the blisters! Instead, pour cold water over the burn or soak it in cold water. The more quickly cold water meets the wound, the sooner the burning effect will be stopped, particularly in the deeper layers of skin. Cover the burn with a sterile bandage.

It is highly unlikely that you'll encounter third-degree burns in the outdoors, but they're easily distinguished from the first two because the flesh is charred. A third-degree burn must be treated in a hospital. Do not remove any clothing that has adhered to the burn. If you can't get to a hospital within an hour, give the victim a weak solution of salt water to sip slowly. This will help replace the essential fluids that were lost because of the burn. Because of the severity of third-degree burns, you should not immerse them in cold water. Do cover the area with a clean cloth and get the victim to a doctor as soon as possible.

Stop, Drop, and Roll

If your clothing should ever catch fire, your natural instinct may be to run. Don't! This will only fuel the flames with oxygen. Instead, drop to the ground immediately, flames to the ground, and roll around in complete circles (depending on the extent of the flames) until the fire has been smothered.

Keep in mind when you sit close to a campfire that today's synthetic fibers (fleece pants and jackets, lycra, etc.) can make burns more dangerous because the material melts into your skin instead of ashing and flaking away.

Fractures

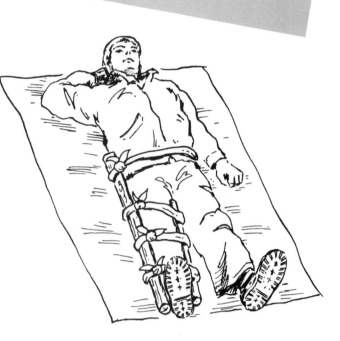

fracture is a serious injury and requires medical attention. If you think someone has broken a bone, check for swelling, discoloration, crookedness, and severe pain. If you are still unsure, it's best to assume that it is a fracture.

Don't attempt to set the broken bone or to straighten it unless the injured limb is bent under the victim and you are several hours from help. If you must move an arm or leg, do so very gently. Cut away any wet clothing so you can keep the victim warm. The injured person will probably be in shock and more susceptible to hypothermia.

If the fracture is of the collarbone, upper arm, elbow, forearm, wrist, finger, ankle, or foot, you may be able to splint the bone. The purpose of splinting is to keep the joint above and below the fracture from moving (unless, of course, it's the joint that's fractured). You can use heavy sticks or tent poles for splints, and bandanas or clothing for padding. Place a stick on either side of the affected limb and tie off above and below the break with several bandanas or strips of cloth. If the victim can walk, get him or her to help as soon as possible.

If the fracture is of a bone other than those listed above, have the victim lie very quietly, and use sleeping bags or clothing to surround the fracture with as much padding as possible. Make sure the victim is warm before you go for help.

Ropework in Camp

A braided or twisted nylon rope can perform a number of important camp functions. You'll need at least one 10-foot-long rope, ⅛ to ¼ inch thick. It's best to use white or light-colored rope that'll be easy to spot in the dark. A length of light-colored nylon cord is useful for guylines, tying up your pack, or rigging a clothesline.

You'll also need a 20-foot-long rope to hang a "smellables" bag in areas where raccoons, mice, bears, or other animals have become campground food poachers. One long rope per group of four is usually enough.

The main parts of the rope are the standing part, or body of the rope, and the free end, at the cut end of the rope. These terms are important for understanding knot-tying descriptions.

Parts of a Knot

All knots are made up of combinations of bights, loops, and overhand knots. A *bight* is made by bending the free end over the standing part until the two are parallel. To form a *loop*, continue bending the free end until it crosses over the standing part. For an *overhand knot*, pull the free end through the loop.

Always leave several inches of the free end extending beyond the finished knot to prevent the knot from slipping loose under strain.

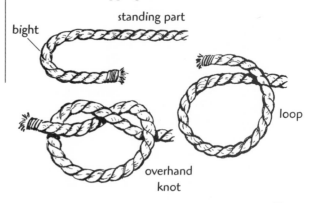

standing part

bight

loop

overhand knot

Knots for Joining Rope

If you have two shorter lengths of rope and need one long rope, these knots will join the two ropes without diminishing their usefulness.

Double Fisherman's Knot

This knot is a double-loop variant of the knot fishermen use to tie two pieces of fine line together. The second loop gives it extra security.

1. Lay the standing parts and free ends of two pieces of rope parallel to each other with the free ends going in opposite directions.

2. Wrap the free end of the first rope twice around the standing part of the second rope, moving away from the second rope's free end.

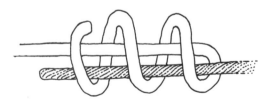

3. Push the free end of the first rope back through the loops you just made and tighten it.

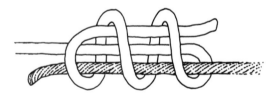

4. Repeat steps 1 to 3 but this time wrap the *second* rope's free end around the *first* rope's standing part; pull the free end back through the loops and tighten it.

5. Pull the standing parts of both ropes to complete the knot.

Sheet Bend

This knot and the double sheet bend variant get their names from sails (sometimes called sheets), not bedcovers. They're good for joining two ropes of unequal thickness.

1. Make a bight in the thicker of the two ropes.

2. Pass the free end of the thinner rope through the middle of the bight.

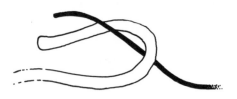

3. Wrap this free end around the back of the bight.

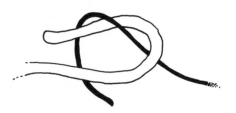

4. Pass the free end under its own standing part and tighten it.

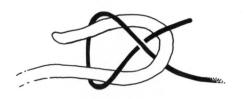

Double Sheet Bend

The double sheet bend is good for joining two slick nylon lines together.

1. Make a bight in the thicker of the two ropes.

2. Pass the free end of the thinner rope through the middle of the bight.

3. Wrap this free end *twice* around *one side* of the bight.

4. Pass the free end under its own standing part and tighten it.

Knots for Attaching

With a hitch you can tie lines to tents and stakes, hang a pack from a tree, hold gear down on the roof of the car, and more. If you're ever stranded on a desert island with the knowledge of only a few knots (It could happen!), at least one of them should be a hitch.

Two Half Hitches

This knot and its quick-release variant are good for tying guylines to grommets and trees.

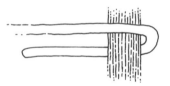

1. Pass the free end of the rope through a grommet or around a tree to form a bight.

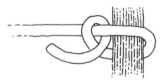

2. Loop the free end over the standing part and pull it up between the grommet or tree and the beginning of the loop.

3. Repeat steps 1 and 2, this time tying the hitch *away* from the grommet or tree.
4. Pull on both the free end and the standing part of the rope at once to tighten the knot.

Two Half Hitches with Quick Release

This knot holds well under strain and comes loose easily with a pull on the free end.

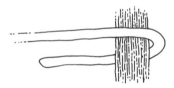

1. Follow steps 1 to 4 above to make two half-hitches.

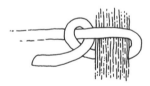

2. Make the quick-release loop by passing the free end of the rope through the second hitch as you tighten the knot down.

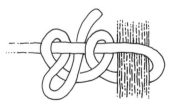

Taut-Line Hitch

This knot slides easily up and down the standing part of the rope, making it easy to adjust the tension on tent stakes, for example. It holds tight under strain and is a good choice for securing the free end of the rope to a tree after hanging a smellables bag.

1. Pass the free end of the rope around a tree or stake to form a bight.

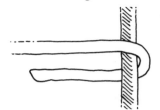

2. Loop the free end twice around the standing part of the rope.

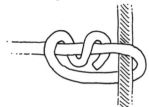

3. Make a third loop around the standing part away from the tree and the first two loops. Pull the free end through this loop to complete the hitch.

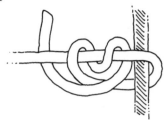

4. Pull the hitch tight and adjust the tension on the standing part.

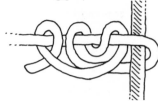

Clove Hitch

The clove hitch is an important knot for lashing (fastening two or more poles together with rope); all lashes begin and end with a clove hitch. It can also be used to tie a line to a tree or post.

1. Loop the rope around a tree with the free end lying over the standing part.

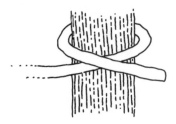

2. Loop the rope around the tree a second time. Pass the free end through this new loop and tighten it.

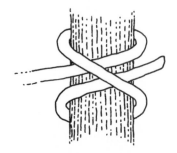

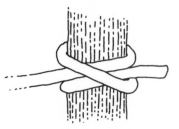

Other Knots

There are hundreds of other knots you can learn, each with a specific purpose. The bowline and miller's knots are included here to round out the selection of knots you're most likely to need for camping and backpacking.

Bowline

The bowline is used to create a loop that won't close in on itself under strain. The time-honored way to remember how to tie a bowline is, "The rabbit comes out of the hole, goes around a tree, sees a fox, and ducks back into the hole." In this saying, the rabbit is the free end of the rope, the hole is the loop, and the tree is the standing part.

1. Make an overhand loop with the standing part of the rope.

2. Push the free end of the rope through this loop.

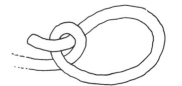

3. Going counterclockwise, wrap the free end behind the standing part, push it back through the loop, and tighten the knot.

Miller's Knot

The miller's knot is the best way to tie a rope around your smellables bag. Millers traditionally used this knot to tie up sacks of grain ground at their grist mill.

1. Make an overhand loop about six inches below the mouth of the bag.

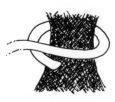

2. Loop the free end around the bag a second time.

3. Pull it through the first overhand loop and tighten it.

Hanging a Smellables Bag

15'

10'

4'-5' drop

All campsites attract animals. Some areas have more problems than others, but you'll always want to prevent animals from breaking into your food supply and other gear. Now is the time to find a tree to hang smellables from. You'll need to hang the bag at least 10 feet off the ground and at least 4 feet from the tree. Don't skimp on distance from the ground or tree. If the campground says it's having problems with animals getting into food, you've got to prepare for attack by a kamikaze raccoon or bear diving from a limb above.

When you make camp you should select the tree and get a rope over a branch so you can get the bag up easily in the dark. Weight a rope with a stick and toss it over the branch you've chosen. Pull hard on both ends of the rope to make sure the branch will hold. Tie one end to the tree and leave the other free to attach to the bag later.

When you're ready to go to bed, pack food and other items whose smells might attract animals (such as toothpaste and soap) into an empty sleeping bag stuff sack. Find a stick roughly 2 inches thick and 1 foot long. Lay the end of the bag over the stick and tie a miller's knot around both sides of the bag beneath the stick. This will keep the bag from sliding out of the knot at night. Pull the bag up at least 10 feet using the long standing part of the rope and tie it off on the tree trunk with a taut-line hitch.

Trouble with Bears

The problem in the Great Smoky Mountains and other national parks isn't the bears—it's the people.

So how much trouble are bears to people? In 1993 there were no people injured in the Smokies but there were 36 incidents of bears damaging property. With hundreds of bears and millions of visitors, it's plain that the problem is small.

Park officials say that if people would follow the rules and leave bears alone, there wouldn't be any incidents to report.

Reading a Topographic Map

A highway map may get you to a state or national park, but once you get there you'll need a topographic (topo) map to find your way around. A topo map gives a two-dimensional picture of our three-dimensional world. It uses *contour lines* to show the land's elevation as well as its length and width. With a topo map and a compass you can find your way in the backcountry and identify landmarks, such as mountains and streams, along the way.

In the United States topographic maps are made by the United States Geological Survey (USGS). In Canada they're produced by the Surveys and Mapping Branch of the Department of Mines and Technical Surveys.

The USGS offers very detailed *quadrangle maps* (or *quads*) of much of the United States. Quads can be found in both 7.5-minute and 15-minute detail. *Minutes* are fractions of degrees of longitude and latitude; 1 degree equals 60 minutes. A 7.5-minute map is 7.5 minutes longitude by 7.5 minutes latitude. The larger the number of minutes, the less detail the map has. The 7.5-minute is the most common and supplies the most detail of any map, showing about 70 square miles or fewer.

USGS maps are available in outdoor stores or directly from the USGS. For maps of areas east of the Mississippi River, write to U.S. Geologic Survey, Washington, DC 20242; west of the Mississippi the address is U.S. Geologic Survey, Federal Center, Denver, CO 80225. Index maps for each state are available free of charge. Order Canadian maps from the Map Distribution Office, Department of Mines and Technical Surveys, Ottawa, Ontario, Canada.

Colors

USGS topo maps use a standard set of colors for features on their maps.

Brown: contour lines, which give the elevation of a given area

Green: areas of vegetation, including fields, orchards, and forests

Blue: water, including springs, streams, lakes, rivers, and oceans

Black: man-made features such as buildings, boundaries, roads, and dams

Red: highways

Yellow: large cities

Symbols

There are dozens of symbols used on topo maps, but these are the most common ones you will find:

□■▨	Building
⌖	Church
⌂	School
[†] [CEM]	Cemetery
blue tint	Lake or pond
≈≈≈	Stream
○~	Spring
▱	Marsh or swamp
- - - - -	Trail
⟩⟩	Bridge
══	Street
▬▬	Highway
= = = =	Gravel road
++++++	Railroad tracks
—·—·—·—	Power line

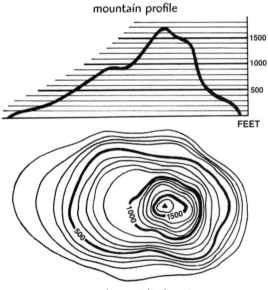

mountain profile

contour lines with elevations

Contour Lines

The irregular brown lines show elevation above sea level. Any point along a given contour line is at the same elevation. The map's legend will tell you the *contour interval* for the map. Always check this number as you orient yourself to a map. One USGS quad may use a 20-foot interval while the adjoining quad uses a 40-foot interval. These numbers mean that each line represents another 20 (or 40) feet above sea level.

Where these lines are close together, the terrain is steep. The farther apart they are, the more moderate the slope.

To find the elevation, look for the *index lines*. These are the thicker brown contour lines that are numbered. On a line numbered 500, for example, everything along that line is 500 feet above sea level. On a map with a 20-foot interval the thin line inside the index line represents 520 feet above sea level and the thin line outside the index line represents 480 feet above sea level.

Scale

The scale for a 7.5-minute quad is 1:24,000. This means that 1 inch on the map represents 24,000 inches (or 2,000 feet) on the ground. A 15-minute map has a scale of 1:62,500, which translates to 1 inch per 5,208 feet, or nearly one mile. Whatever the scale of the map you use, its legend will include a *bar scale* showing the length of different straight-line distances—miles, kilometers, and nautical miles—relative to the map's scale.

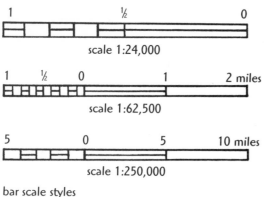

bar scale styles

Map Date

In the bottom right corner of USGS maps you'll find a date or a series of dates. One map might be dated just 1958, for example, which would tell you that the map was made in 1958 and that none of the information is more recent than that year. Another map might read, "1949, Aerial Photography 1972," which would tell you that the map was originally made in 1949 and supplemented with information from a 1972 aerial survey. You will find only the most up-to-date maps in stores, but the date will let you know how current the information on the map is. A 20-year-old map would be unreliable for information on buildings and roads, but should still have good topographic detail. An old map, however, may not show a new dam on a river or a swamp that has since been drained.

Measuring Distance on a Map

To measure a certain linear distance, lay a piece of paper over the map. Mark one tick on the paper at the starting point of that distance, and another tick at the end point. Lay the paper along the map's bar scale and read the distance.

You can figure out a nonlinear distance, such as a length of river, on a topo map using a similar method. Mark the first point on a sheet of paper as before. Now slant the paper to follow the bends in the river, marking ticks at significant turns until you reach the end point. Read the total distance against the bar scale. It's even easier to measure nonlinear distance with a piece of string, but make sure the string you use doesn't stretch.

Another way to measure is to make a ruler for your map by laying your paper along the bar scale. Put one end of the paper at one end of the mile scale. Mark a tick at the 0, which is in the middle of the scale, and another tick at the 1-mile mark. This will give you a two-mile ruler to measure linear distances on your map.

"To those devoid of imagination, a blank place on the map is a useless waste; to others, the most valuable part."

—Aldo Leopold, *A Sand County Almanac*

Using a Compass

A compass is essential to understanding and using a map; you'll need it to orient your map and find your way. The compass is much more than the magnetized needle it houses. It's marked with the cardinal points of north, south, east, and west, and with the degrees of a circle starting with 0 and working clockwise to 359 (360 degrees is also the 0 mark). A good compass has a revolving needle housing on a clear baseplate.

Magnetic North

The compass doesn't point to true north, but rather to magnetic north. This magnetic north pole, where all magnetic lines of force converge, moves slightly from year to year. It's currently in northern Canada, about 1,400 miles south of the true North Pole.

Maps, on the other hand, are oriented to true north. To compensate for this, maps are marked with the *magnetic declination* and the year that declination was accurate. For most purposes, the annual change in the magnetic declination won't affect how you find your way.

In North America the line of no declination (or *agonic line*) extends from Wisconsin down to the tip of Florida. In northern Maine the declination is about 20 degrees west. (Add the degrees of declination to your compass reading for a true reading.) The declination in Oregon is about 20 degrees east. (Subtract the degrees of declination for a true reading.) The greater the declination, the farther off your bearings will be if you orient your map to true north instead of magnetic north.

Orienting Your Map

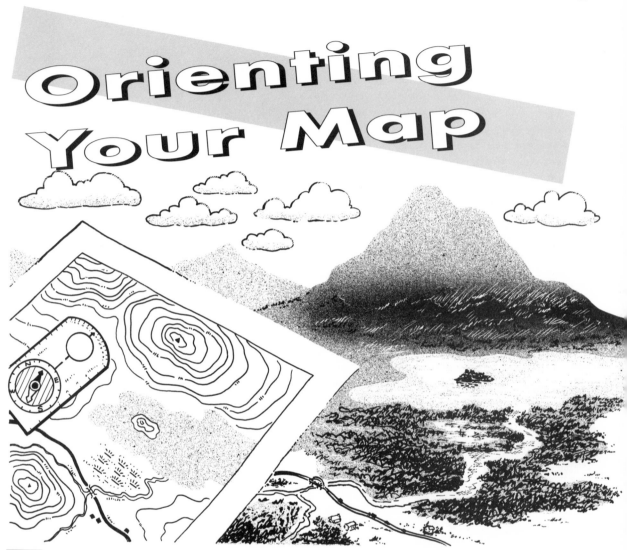

The simple way to orient your map is to use known landmarks. First, find where you are on the map and locate a landmark (such as a mountain peak) both on the map and on the ground. Now turn the map so that the landmark on the map is in the same direction as the landmark on the ground. This will give you a rough idea of where things are on the map and it's a quick way to identify landmarks you don't recognize without using a compass.

For wayfinding and orienteering you will need to use a compass. Spread out your map and lay your compass on top of it. With your compass adjusted for declination, turn its dial so that the line for direction of travel is at north. Align the baseplate of the compass with the edge of the map. Make sure the line of travel is toward the top of the map. Turn the map to align the compass needle within the orienting arrow's outline. Now the map is oriented and you can find your location on the map.

To adjust your compass for declination, rotate the center of the compass case so that the orienting arrow is offset from north by the amount of your local declination.

Taking Compass Bearings

A bearing is a direction given in compass degrees. Let's say you're standing at a viewpoint in the mountains. You want to determine the bearing to all the visible mountain peaks from this viewpoint. To do this, point the direction-of-travel arrow on your compass at the object you wish to get a bearing on, hold the compass level, and turn the revolving ring that houses the north arrow until the alignment arrow matches up with the north arrow. The bearing to the landmark is the degree number at the base of the direction-of-travel arrow.

You can use a bearing to identify landmarks on a map by taking a bearing and following that angle of travel on the map from the point you're standing at until it crosses a feature on the ground that matches the landmark on the map. It will be easy to mistake a landmark on the ground for the wrong feature on the map, but you can double-check your work by noting other topographic features around the landmark you just identified to see that they match up with the area on the map surrounding your landmark.

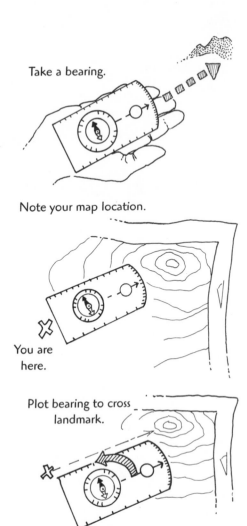

Take a bearing.

Note your map location.

You are here.

Plot bearing to cross landmark.

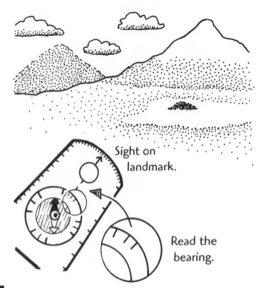

Sight on landmark.

Read the bearing.

Bearings can also help you determine the direction of travel you need to get out of a wilderness when you're lost. First, look at your map and determine your likely location. Second, find a nearby road on the map. Take compass bearings that will have you cross that road, and follow your compass in that direction by aligning the direction-of-travel arrow with that bearing while keeping the magnetized needle aligned with the alignment arrow. Continue hiking in that direction until you reach the road. However, you should never follow a compass bearing away from an established trail or campground. If you get in trouble you'll be found more quickly if you stay put and wait for help to come to you.

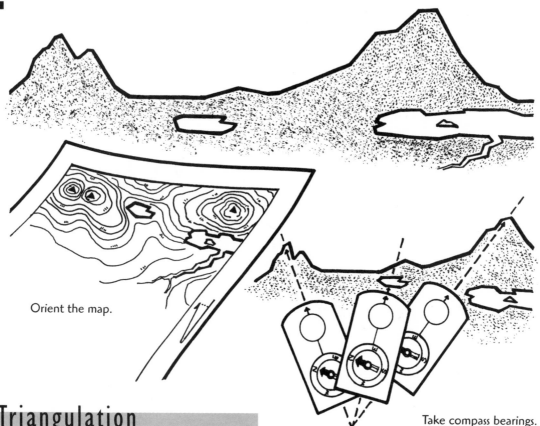

Orient the map.

Take compass bearings.

Triangulation

What if you're not sure where you are? With a topo map and a compass you can use triangulation to determine your position on the map. First, orient the map and determine your approximate position. Now look for landmarks you can identify on the map. Determine the bearing for a landmark and use a ruler to mark a line on the map from the landmark, following the compass bearing, back to your assumed location and beyond. Do the same for a second landmark at least 45 degrees away from the first. This second line should cross the first at your current position. To verify your position, take a bearing on a third landmark between the first two and draw a line on the map along its path. This third mark should cross at or very close to the intersection of the first two lines and verify your position. You can use this technique to make maps, find your way back to a favorite fishing hole on a lake, or determine any fixed position on a map.

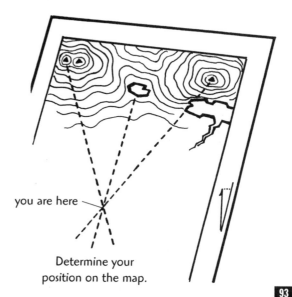

you are here

Determine your position on the map.

Making an orienteering course

There are lots of games you can be play using a compass, with or without a map. Orienteering games are a good way to hone your map and compass skills. To set up a compass course for group competition you'll need a wooded park or similar area of at least 2 acres, a black magic marker, 10 sheets of paper, some thumbtacks, and a compass.

1. From the starting point, take a compass bearing to a tree at least 20 yards away.

2. Pace off the distance to that tree and write down the bearing and the number of paces on a sheet of paper.

3. Take a bearing on a second tree at least 20 yards away, pace off that distance, and write the bearing and number of paces on a second sheet of paper.

4. Continue until you have 10 points on a course that leads back to the starting point. The course should cross over itself from time to time.

START

FINISH

5. Tack up the first sheet of paper, which gives the compass bearing and number of paces to the first tree, at the starting point. Test your directions by following the bearing and pacing the distance to the tree. If your directions are wrong, try it again and correct the bearing or number of paces.

6. Tack the directions for the second leg of the course on the first tree so that it can't be seen as you approach from the starting point. Continue following the course and tacking up the sheets of paper.

When you're finished, send competitors over the course and time how long it takes them to reach the end. The person with the shortest time wins.

Reading Mountain Terrain

Dangers in the backcountry aren't always as obvious as the carrion breath of a mama grizzly roaring in your face as she protects her cubs. Death and dismemberment can be lurking in a rock pile, snow-laden ridgetop, or sparkling stream if you don't know what to look for and how to avoid the dangers.

Talus/Scree

Between steep, rocky mountain slopes and valleys is a rock-choked middle ground of boulders, known as talus, and smaller fragments, called scree. The talus slopes of older mountains are filled in with dirt and plant life. On other newer mountains, the stones can be loose and provide an unstable path for hikers. Take care on talus slopes, testing each rock before committing your weight to it. Be ready to hop to a more stable boulder if the one you're on rolls loose. No matter how careful you are on scree, you will send rocks tumbling downhill. Groups are better off climbing scree together, so no one is left downhill in the path of sliding rocks.

Avalanche Danger

No one knows when an avalanche will strike. The right amount of snow, angle of slope, and the proper weather conditions will send truck-loads of snow thundering down a mountain,

Leeward slopes:
Prevailing mountain winds drive snow to the opposite side of the mountaintop. These leeward slopes build up deep cornices of snow along the ridgetop. These cornices pose the greatest avalanche danger.

Recent heavy snowfall:
Danger is highest the first three days after the snow falls.

Slope angle:
A mountainside steeper than 30 degrees, but less than 45 degrees, poses the greatest risk.

Open or lightly forested slopes.

Look for these indicators of danger

ripping through everything in its path, burying the mountainside in a thick white shroud. Knowing the conditions that lead to an avalanche will help you steer around its path without having to worry.

Stay in zones of travel that pose the least risk of avalanche danger. These include the windward side of the ridgetop away from the cornices of snow on the leeward slope, the middle of the valley, and heavily forested slopes, whose trees anchor the snow.

Avalanches often occur repeatedly on the same slopes. These avalanche chutes have no or few trees. The trees you see in the area will often be scarred with snow-ripped branches. If your group must traverse an area prone to avalanches, particularly after heavy snowfalls, do so early in the morning and go one at a time, roped to other members of your group who watch and belay your traverse. Unfasten your pack's waist belt and be ready to ditch your gear in an avalanche. If you are caught in an avalanche, pull your way through the snow, swimming toward the surface. As the snow slows, hold a hand in front of your face to create a space of air to breathe in. Push a hand up to try to reach the surface and wait for your partners to dig you out.

Stream Crossings

Fording streams doesn't just mean splashing across a shallow creek. You may have to contend with a thigh-deep slog through a swift stream. Most trails ford streams at the best location in the area, but if the crossing is more than ankle deep, you may want to scout up and downstream for a shallower route.

You may be tempted to pull off your boots and ford the stream barefooted, but this often results in an embarrassing dunk in a cold creek. You'll need to have the traction boots or shoes offer to stay up on the slick, rounded stones that lie on the streambed. A dry alternative is to switch to river sandals or tennis shoes for the crossing and back to boots on the other side.

Unhitch the waist belt on your pack so you can slip out of it easily if you go under water. Use a hiking stick for balance, even if you don't normally carry one (find a good downed limb nearby if possible). Your feet and the stick form three points for balance. In swift or deep water, move only one of the three points at a time to maintain control.

If you get knocked under water, slip out of your pack and try to get back up and continue. If the current makes it hard to regain footing, swim to the bank and look for your pack. It will be easier to find the pack from the shore of a clear stream than while wading.

Mountain Biking

Gently rolling along a mountain trail, you pause to admire a fern frond before slowly peddling on. *Not!* Let's face it, the grueling uphills are OK, but nothing beats screaming down the mountain with the forest a blur all around you.

Still, it's essential to stay in control of your bike on rough terrain. Always be aware of others using the trail; be prepared to slow down and leave room for hikers, horseback riders, and even other bikers. "Hammerheads"— bikers who ignore other trail users in their search for the extreme—have done a lot to alienate hikers and horseback riders. If you're polite and you maintain control, maybe you'll repair the mountain biker's reputation.

Wear a helmet at all times and carry plenty of water to keep hydrated during your ride.

Climbing

On a steep uphill, gearing and balance can keep you pumping pedals when others are walking their bikes. Switch to a low gear before the slope steepens. Your legs should be turning quickly at the bottom of a big hill. With a low gear, even one that seems too low, your bike will be able to react to obstacles without losing speed.

Balance is crucial on uphill sections of trail. Maintain a low center of gravity by standing up on the pedals; this shifts your weight from the seat to the pedals themselves. Lean forward to keep your front wheel on the ground. When the trail gets even steeper, dismount and push the bike.

Braking

On the trail you'll use your brakes to keep your speed under control more than for actually stopping. To maintain control, brake on smooth, dry ground, and slow down on straightaways *before* you enter turns. Using the front brake in a turn is asking for a crash, but braking hard on the rear brake can cause you to fishtail.

On rough trail you may not need to brake as often as instinct tells you to. Keeping an even speed over small obstacles will make the going smoother.

Carrying Your Bike

Occasionally you'll have to carry your bike through streams, over logs, and around other obstructions. Keep the side with the chain and gears exposed away from your body as you portage your bike–gear teeth can make nasty divots in your skin.

Downhill

Getting back down a mountain quickly and safely is the greatest test of a mountain biker's skill—balance is perhaps more important here than on uphill stretches. Maintain control by shifting your weight to the back of the bike. Sit with your rump edging over the back of the seat, your arms fully extended to grip the handlebars, and your fingers over the brake levers.

Canoeing

Canoeing rivals backpacking as the simplest way to travel, and it's fun for either a short trip around a pond or an extended backcountry paddle. Whether it's gliding among alligators in a southern swamp, or moose in a northern lake, the canoe is quiet enough for observing wildlife not seen on developed shores. A few basic skills and pieces of equipment are all you need.

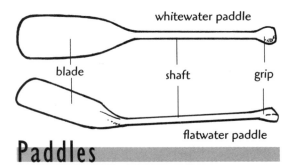

whitewater paddle

blade   shaft   grip

flatwater paddle

Paddles

The canoe holds you up in the water, but it's the paddle that gets you where you want to go. It's important to find a well-built paddle that fits your canoeing style and body size. Bent-shaft paddles are more efficient for flatwater paddling; straight-shaft paddles are made for whitewater. The grip should be wider than your palm and should fit comfortably in your hand.

To measure a paddle for size, sit upright on a chair or bench. With the grip of the paddle resting on the seat between your legs, the point where the shaft meets the blade should be at eye level. If you sit up on the seat of a canoe instead of kneeling on the floor, you may want the shaft to be a few inches longer.

Safety Gear

Each paddler must wear a lifejacket (also known as a personal flotation device, or PFD) made of closed-cell foam sewn into a synthetic liner. The lifejacket should be broad enough to fit over bulky clothes, yet adjustable to fit when you're wearing only a swimsuit, and rated to support your weight.

A 50-foot rescue line and a helmet for each paddler are required equipment for canoeing on whitewater.

The Canoe

Each canoe is designed with a particular use in mind. The bottom of a short whitewater canoe is shaped like a rocking chair to make it ride high and maneuver easily. Long, flat-bottomed touring canoes give you room for gear and are designed for flatwater paddling.

Whatever the size and style of your canoe, its basic parts are the same as on any boat. The front of the canoe is the *bow* and the rear is the *stern*. The left side is *port* and the right side is *starboard*. Toward the bow or in front of the canoe is *fore*; toward the rear or behind the canoe is *aft*.

Getting In and Out

You're more likely to get dunked in the water while getting in and out of the canoe than when you're paddling. To get into a canoe from a dock, have your paddling partner hold the canoe firmly against the dock while you climb in. Hold onto the closest *gunwale* (the upper edge of a boat's side, pronounced "gunnel") with one hand and set one foot down a few inches beyond the center of the canoe. Bring the second foot in parallel to the first and grip both gunwales. Keep your weight low as you move to your seat. Once you're settled, hold the dock so the second paddler can climb in. Follow these steps in reverse when you return to the dock.

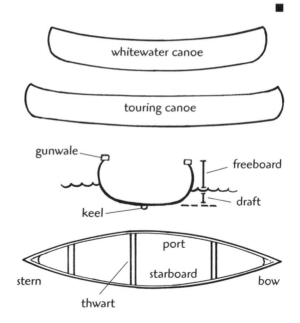

To board from land, point the canoe out into the water with the stern against the shore. The stern paddler holds the canoe firmly between the knees and grips both gunwales. The bow paddler steps slowly into the center of the boat and moves forward to the bow seat, keeping low and holding the gunwales. The stern paddler pushes the canoe out about a foot from shore, if possible. The bow paddler holds the canoe steady by pushing a paddle against the river or lake bottom while the stern paddler steps in.

Bow Stroke

This straight-line stroke is the mainstay of the bow paddler. It's used to provide power for the boat while the stern paddler steers. Reach forward with the full face of the paddle blade facing aft. Pull back with your lower hand as you push forward on the grip. Follow through until your lower arm is comfortably straight. Keep the paddle perpendicular to the water as you reach forward for the next stroke. Always keep your arms as straight as possible and use your torso to complete the stroke.

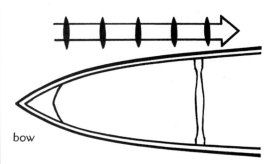

bow

J-Stroke

Begin with a straight pull as in the bow stroke but move the paddle outward as it passes by your body. A solo paddler can use this stroke to keep the canoe on a straight course, and a stern paddler can use it for minor course corrections.

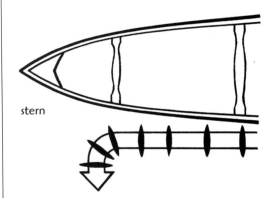

stern

Paddling

Kneel down on the floor of the boat whenever you're on whitewater or in rough weather. If you sit up on a seat or a *thwart* (the supporting bench across a boat) you'll raise your center of gravity and make the canoe easier to tip over. Begin all strokes with one hand on the paddle grip and the other hand a shoulder's width down the shaft.

A few basic strokes will be all you need to get started. Every paddler should know how to do the bow stroke, the J-stroke, the sweep, and the draw. Each paddler can stroke on one side to keep the canoe on course, although you might want to swap sides occasionally to rest your muscles.

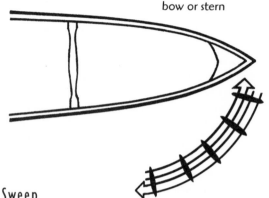

bow or stern

Sweep

This stroke turns the canoe around. Reach forward with the paddle blade parallel to the canoe and plant it into the water. Now pull the paddle back in a wide arc. With a *reverse sweep* you can turn the canoe in the opposite direction without switching the side you paddle on. Begin a reverse sweep with the paddle parallel to the boat, with the face aft. Pull back on the grip and arc the paddle blade forward.

To turn slowly, the bow paddler sweeps while the stern paddler continues with a forward stroke. If one paddler sweeps in one direction while the second paddler sweeps in the opposite direction, the canoe will turn on a dime and leave change to spare.

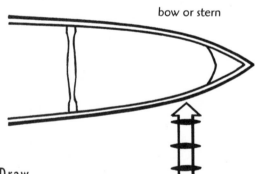

bow or stern

Draw

To pull the canoe close up to a dock, plant the paddle straight into the water at arm's length with the blade parallel to the canoe. Pull the paddle toward the boat, keeping a reasonable distance between the paddle and the canoe so you don't tip over.

Canoe Rescue

Knowing what to do when your canoe is swamped will give you extra confidence on the water. If you get dumped out of a canoe, find your paddle and climb back in. To do this, reach across to the far gunwale with one hand while you push the near gunwale about 6 inches underwater with the other hand. Slide over the near gunwale into the boat, sit down, and bail out as much water as you can. If this is impossible, slowly paddle the water-filled canoe to shore. A canoe will float at gunwale-level even when it's full of water.

If you fall out of a canoe in whitewater you'll have to swim without your boat until you reach calm water. It's important that you stay upstream of the canoe to avoid a worse accident. Keep your feet pointed downstream and your head up out of the water. Work your way to the bank as soon as you safely can.

Canoe Camping

The gear you'll need for a canoe camping trip is almost the same as that listed on pages 6 and 7 for an overnight hike. Instead of a backpack you'll use a dry bag to carry your gear. For the occasional canoe trip you can get by with packing all your gear in a duffle bag lined with a double layer of big trash bags twist-tied to keep the water out. There's a little more room in the bottom of a canoe than in a backpack, but the less gear you carry, the better you canoe trip will be.

A canoe must be loaded properly to keep it from tipping easily. The center of gravity should be near the middle of the boat, so you should settle your packs in the middle and shift them closer to the front or back depending on the weight of the paddlers. For example, if the paddler in the rear weighs more than the pad-

dler in front, the gear should be closer to the front to balance the weight.

Keep all gear as low as possible to maintain the canoe's natural stability and to avoid wind resistance. If you must crawl over your luggage to get in or out of the boat, keep as low as possible and hold on to both gunwales for support.

Selecting a good minimum-impact campsite is tougher on a river trip than on a backpacking trip because all of your potential sites will be closer to water. Rivers flood their banks from time to time and carry buried items downstream. This is why packing out all human waste has become common practice along some rivers, even though it's considered extreme for most camping and backpacking trips.

Reading a River

You can read the story of the riverbed on the surface of the water. If you know what to look for, you can pick the best route through whitewater. The following are some of the features you'll find in rapids up through Class III:

Eddy

An eddy is an area behind a large rock, a ledge, or a tree where the current swirls back upstream. Steer clear of eddies unless you want to "eddy out," or pull into the eddy to take a break after negotiating a rapid.

Pillows and Holes

As water pours over rocks and logs it creates either a pillow upstream or a hole on the downstream side. A pillow is a bulging wave you can ride over easily. A hole is a depression or deep pit where the water rolls in on itself after crashing over the rock. Large rocks can create "keeper" hydraulics on the downstream side that spin your boat through the current until you're thoroughly "Maytagged." Stay away from holes in a canoe.

Ledges

A rock ledge running perpendicular to the current creates a serious hole and should be scouted before you try to run it. There's often an open channel alongside a ledge that makes a safer route to run.

Riffles

Low standing waves created by a shallow, uneven river bottom are known as riffles. It's best to take the deeper channel around these minor obstacles to avoid bottoming out on the rocks.

Strainers

A tree with lots of branches strains the water through and pulls canoeists from their boats. Give strainers a wide berth.

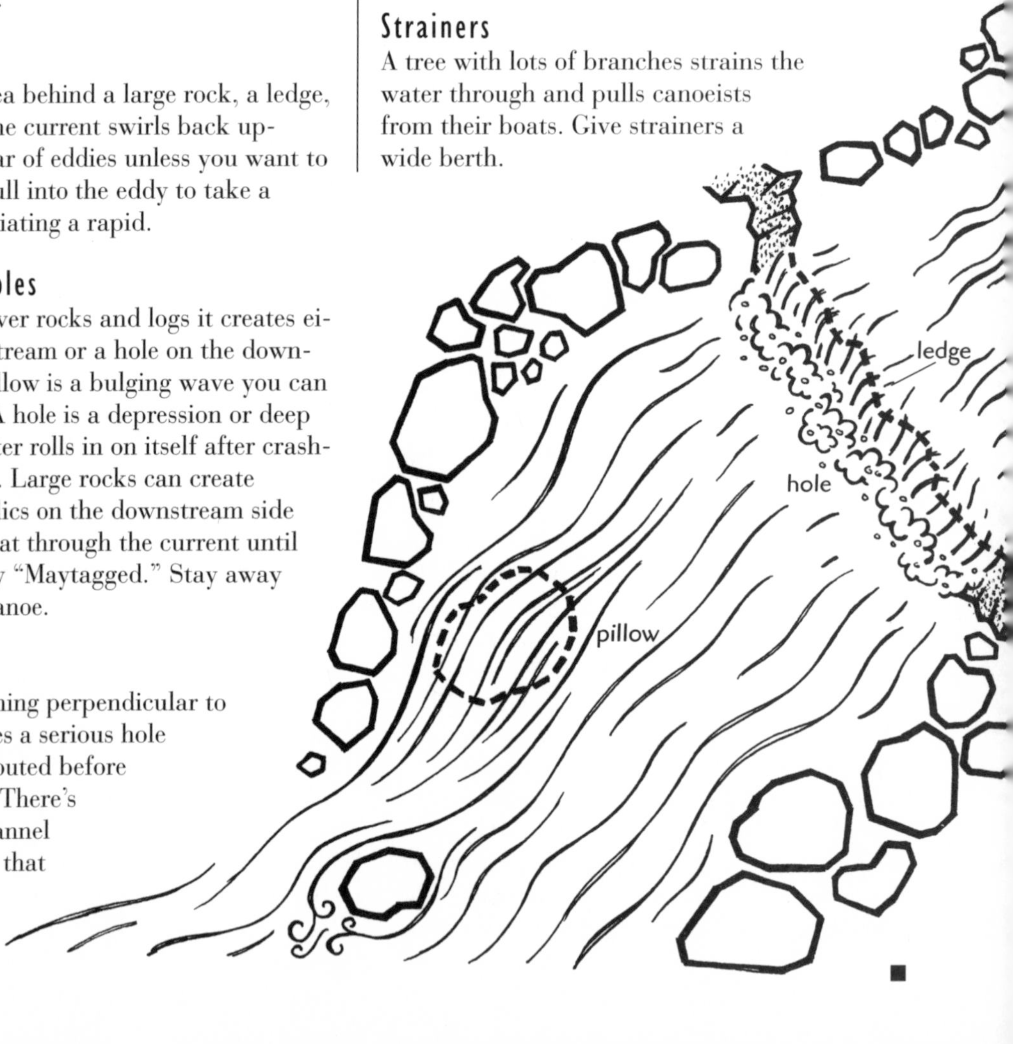

ledge

hole

pillow

Vs

As the channel runs between two obstacles it forms a downstream-pointed V. If you run through the heart of the V, toward the point, you'll follow the deepest water downstream. An upstream-pointed V is created by an exposed or shallow rock or limb. Avoid the tip of an upstream V because it points to an obstacle just breaking the water's surface.

eddy

downstream V

strainer

riffles

Class Ratings

The American White-water Affiliation has produced an American version of the system used worldwide to rate rapids. With a little practice you can learn to handle Class I and II rapids in an open canoe. After plenty of experience on these smaller riffles and waves you'll be able to master Class III rapids.

Class I

These easy rapids are limited to fast-moving waters with small waves. The few obstacles are easily spotted and avoided.

Class II

Good boat-handling skills are more important in these rapids, which feature moderate waves and rocks. Class II rapids have broad channels that can be run without scouting ahead.

Class III

Complex maneuvering is often required to run these rapids with fast currents and irregular waves. Any strainers are easy to bypass. Always scout Class III rapids when you're paddling an open canoe.

Class IV

These adrenaline-pumping rapids are for advanced paddlers. Expect tight channels that require precision and skill. Have a spotter with a rescue line ready when you run these heavy hydraulics.

Class V

Intense rapids with large waves, lots of "keeper" holes, few eddies, and long distances between calm pools. Class V whitewater is run by groups of expert paddlers who have solid rescue skills. Scouting is mandatory.

Class VI

These bone-crushing rapids are the extreme of what humans can run. A false move can result in severe injury or death; rescue is difficult or impossible.

Survival

The word *survival* conjures an image of a plane crash in the Andes Mountains or the Mojave Desert, the survivor catching food with a snare or drinking water out of a cactus. In reality, most survival situations begin with one or more people miscalculating their own abilities and getting lost or stuck outdoors. Survival situations—from the small child wandering away from the campground, to the well-prepared group trapped by an unexpected snow storm in the Rockies—can be life threatening. But they are almost always resolved in 24 hours or less.

Avoiding Survival Situations

To avoid spending unplanned nights in the wilderness, make an itinerary for your trip. Know which trails you'll hike, which campsites you'll sleep at, and when you'll return. Give this itinerary to someone before you leave and follow it on the trip. If you don't return on time, searchers will be able to look for you on the trails and at the campsites you planned to use. If you need help it will take only hours, not days, for someone to find you.

Rapid changes in the weather are often responsible for survival situations. Check the weather for the area you'll be hiking right up until you leave. Prepare yourself with clothes, shelter, food, and sleeping bags appropriate for the extremes you may face.

Getting off an established trail and bush-whacking in search of help will make a rescuer's job very difficult. Attempt this only if you're familiar with the area and a member of your group needs emergency help fast (such as after a serious injury).

Getting Found

To get found you just need to stay put on an established trail or in a designated campsite. Be prepared to signal help if the opportunity arises. One signal is to blow a whistle with the Morse code distress signal "SOS": three short blasts, three long blasts, and three short blasts. In remote areas you can use a mirror to flash sunlight at airplanes to signal for help.

If your partner is injured at a spot away from the trail or campsite, mark the way to the spot to make the searcher's job easier.

Enemies of Survival

If you have to spend an unexpected night or two in the backcountry your main enemies will be thirst, hunger, the weather, and fear. Prepare yourself to deal with these challenges. If you still have your backpack (or daypack in the case of a day hike gone wrong), you should have a canteen and some way to treat water. Drinking water frequently will keep you well hydrated and lessen the danger of your situation. If no water is available, cut back on the amount of water your body is using by staying out of the heat and not exerting yourself.

You should always have one extra meal in your backpack in case of an emergency. The freeze-dried meals sold in backpacking stores are ideal for this because they're lightweight and have extremely long shelf lives. On a day hike, carry some spare candy bars or other snacks in your daypack. These will be enough to keep your energy up while you wait for help.

Extremes in the weather can turn a bad situation into a struggle to survive. The first line of defense against severe weather is to wear clothes that keep you warm when wet and to carry rain gear whether you think you need it or not. Stay dry to keep warmer, and build a fire if cold does settle in. Waterproof matches and fire starter will make it easier to start a fire in wet weather.

If you're dealing with extreme heat you need to keep your body temperature down. Stay in the shade, drink plenty of fluids, and avoid unnecessary exertion.

The last enemy—fear—is perhaps the greatest. Keep a grip on yourself and think your actions all the way through; getting panicky will only make things worse. Knowing how to deal with thirst, hunger, and the weather will greatly lessen your fears.

Shelter

Next to water, shelter is the greatest necessity of life. You can die of exposure before succumbing to starvation. If you're equipped for an overnight trip you should already have a tent or tarp with you, but if you're stranded on a day trip into the backcountry you may have to improvise. First look for natural shelter, such as an overhanging rock ledge. Whether you need shelter from the sun, rain, snow, or wind, a simple lean-to will suffice. A piece of plastic is, of course, preferable for the roof, but vegetation can work too. Face the back of the lean-to into the wind for cold and wet weather.

Survival Kit

A few essential pieces of survival gear will better prepare you for survival situations. Carry this small kit, along with extra food, in addition to the other gear you pack for canoeing, backpacking, mountain biking, and other wilderness ventures. These items will make it easier for rescuers to find you and will help you deal with some of the other problems you'll encounter in one or two unplanned nights in the backcountry.

Plastic whistle

Five foot-long strips of international orange plastic, like that used by surveyors to mark boundary stakes (to mark the way to a member of your group)

Shatterproof signal mirror

Waterproof matches and lighter

Several cotton balls coated with petroleum jelly (for fire starter), carried in a plastic 35 mm film canister

Six iodine tablets (to purify water)

Dry, compressed sponge (to coax moisture out of cracks in rock and other places where a cup can't be dipped)

Solar blanket (lightweight metallic material whose reflective surface retains warmth and provides a signal "blanket")

Clouds

thunderhead

cumulus

stratocumulus

At home, the TV provides regular forecasts to keep you posted on changes in the weather. Watching the weather map and listening to the forecast give you a good guess at what's happening with the weather over the next several days. In the outdoors, a little knowledge of conditions and weather signs can help you predict changes as well.

One important way to keep up with the weather is to learn the differences among cloud patterns and shapes. Cloud facts will help you understand and predict the weather more accurately.

The three main clouds types are *cirrus* (feathered), *stratus* (layered), and *cumulus* (big heaps). These terms are used separately and together, and combined with the terms *nimbus* (rainy) and *alto* (high) to describe cloud cover.

Cirrus clouds appear in long, wispy streaks. They're high-altitude, ice-crystal clouds that often precede a storm front by 24 to 48 hours.

Cirrocumulus clouds are sometimes called mackerel scales because the profusion of small fluffy clouds dotting the sky resembles fish scales. Like their fluffier altocumulus cousins, they're short lived. Cirrocumulus clouds warn of a coming change in the weather, often appearing before rain showers.

Cumulus clouds are immense white clouds that twist and turn into new shapes as they

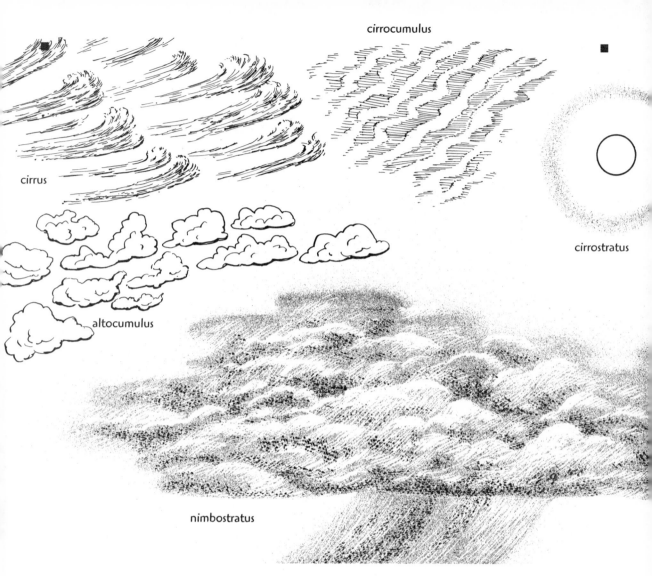

cirrocumulus

cirrus

altocumulus

cirrostratus

nimbostratus

drift across the sky. They're pretty to look at and don't always foretell bad weather. When cumulus clouds congregate they form impressive *thunderheads*, which are breeding grounds for electrical storms, hail, and flash floods.

In the course of an afternoon, docile cumulus clouds can morph into their evil twin—cumulonimbus, or raining cumulus clouds. They create violent but highly localized storms that can pass quickly by, sometimes only to form again for another assault.

Altocumulus clouds look like cotton balls spread across a blue sky. These high-altitude clouds are short lived and predict fair weather.

Stratocumulus clouds are layers of gray clouds that often form into stratus clouds. Stratus clouds are also created by a sequence that begins with cirrus clouds, followed by cirrostratus that thinly veil the sun. As the front moves in, altostratus clouds form a denser layer of gray across the sky. Stratus clouds will soon blot out the sky with a layer of gray. The rain will follow in 5 to 7 hours as the clouds become nimbostratus. These clouds have staying power and produce long, soaking rains with no violent thunderstorms.

Weather Forecasting Signs

There are many signs that indicate changes in the weather. Old sayings like "Red sky at night, sailors delight; red sky in the morning, sailors take warning," all have a basis in fact. You can astound your friends by using the wind, temperature, clouds, and barometer readings to forecast the weather fairly accurately.

Fair Weather

1. Wind blows from the west to the northwest.
2. The barometer stays steady or rises.
3. Morning fog burns off by noon.
4. Cumulus clouds float in the sky in the afternoon.

Rain or Snow

1. Cirrus clouds build and are followed by low clouds.
2. Cumulus clouds build vertically.
3. To the west, the sky becomes dark and threatening.
4. A south wind increases in speed and clouds move in from the west.
5. The wind, especially if it's from the north, shifts in a counterclockwise direction.
6. The barometer falls steadily.
7. You see a ring around the moon.

Clearing Weather

1. Cloud bases rise to higher types.
2. The wind, especially if it's from the east, shifts to the west.
3. The barometer rises rapidly.

Falling Temperatures

1. Wind blows in from or shifts to the north or northwest.
2. There is a clear night sky with a light wind.
3. In winter the barometer rises steadily.

Rising Temperatures

There is a south wind with a cloud cover at night or a clear sky during the day.

Make a weather station

There are three tools you can build that will help you to learn the principles of meteorology and to predict the weather: a barometer, a wind vane, and a rain gauge. Another necessary item, which you'll have to buy, is a thermometer that gives both the highest and the lowest temperature.

Weather Records

Most Rain in a Day: 73.62 inches, Reunion in the Indian Ocean, March 15, 1952

Most Snow in a Day: 75.8 inches, Silver Lake in Colorado, April 14–15, 1921

Fastest Wind Speed: 231 mph, on top of Mount Washington in New Hampshire, April 12, 1934

Biggest Hailstone: 17.5 inches, Coffeyville, Kansas, September 3, 1979

Highest Temperature: 136 degrees Fahrenheit, Azizia in Tripolitania, Libya, September 13, 1922

Lowest Temperature: −129 degrees Fahrenheit, Vostok in Antarctica, July 21, 1983

Barometer

You will need:
- a 12-ounce, straight-necked, clear glass bottle
- an 18-ounce clear glass jar
- water
- food coloring
- a rubber band

1. The bottle must be able to sit neck down in the jar without touching the bottom of the jar. Look for a bottle with rounded shoulders (such as a vinegar bottle) and a mayonnaise or pickle jar. Clean them and remove their labels. Set the bottle neck-down into the jar.
2. Fill the jar with enough water to cover the mouth of the bottle by an inch or so. Add a few drops of food coloring (your preference) and tip the bottle and jar so that some of the air escapes from the bottle in bubbles.
3. Slide the rubber band around the jar and set it at water level, moving it as the water level rises and falls. Place the barometer in a safe place out of direct sunlight.

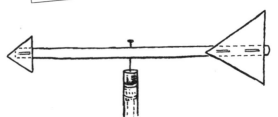

Wind Vane

You will need:
- a plastic milk jug
- scissors
- a stapler
- a straw
- a pin
- a pencil with an eraser

1. Cut two triangles out of the milk jug. Make one triangle slightly smaller than the other.
2. Staple the small triangle to one end of the straw to act as the point of the wind vane, and the larger triangle to the other end for the tail. Make sure both triangles are pointing in the same direction.
3. Push the pin through the center of the straw and into the eraser at the top of the pencil.

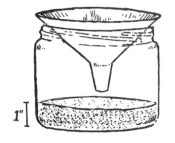

Rain Gauge

You will need:

    a metal or plastic funnel

    a wide-mouthed jar with straight sides, the same
        diameter as the funnel

    a tall, thin jar with straight sides

    masking tape

    a pen

1. Pour an inch of water into the wide-mouthed jar.
   Measure it.
2. Pour the same amount of water into the narrow jar.
3. Stick a length of masking tape down the side of the
   narrow jar and make a mark at the water level.
   This is an "inch."
4. Divide this inch into eight equal parts. Using the same
   measurement as the first inch, mark consecutive inches
   on the bottle and break each one into eight parts.
5. The larger jar, with the funnel set in its mouth, is the
   collection jar. The narrow jar is the measuring jar.

Rain Game

The next time it rains, put out a pan filled with 2
inches of flour. Wait a few minutes and then bring the
pan inside. Let the flour dry for about 3 hours and
then sift out the hardened flour pellets. Arrange them
by size. The smallest pellets fell the farthest to Earth.

Weather Station

You will need:

    a milk crate or other ventilated box

    the thermometer mentioned earlier

    your homemade weather instruments

    lined paper

    graph paper

    a pencil

    a sealable plastic bag.

1. Locate a spot near your home where you can leave your
   crate in an unobstructed area.
2. Hang the thermometer inside the crate, making sure it's
   never in direct sunlight. Attach your wind vane and
   rain gauge. The barometer stays inside your house.

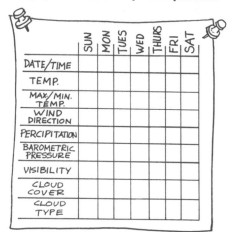

	SUN	MON	TUES	WED	THURS	FRI	SAT
DATE/TIME							
TEMP.							
MAX/MIN. TEMP.							
WIND DIRECTION							
PERCIPITATION							
BAROMETRIC PRESSURE							
VISIBILITY							
CLOUD COVER							
CLOUD TYPE							

3. Make a weather conditions chart. Draw seven columns
   for the days of the week, and eight lines for entries.
   The entries are: date and time, present temperature,
   minimum/maximum temperature, wind direction, precipitation, barometric pressure, visibility, amount of
   cloud cover, and cloud type. Leave a space for a forecast at the bottom. Make multiple copies of your chart.
4. Make a rain chart. On graph paper, write the dates for
   the next couple of weeks along the bottom, and
   inches of precipitation along the left side.
5. Store your charts in the plastic bag and choose a consis-
   tent time to make measurements—early in the day
   is best.
6. The first day you take readings, leave the minimum/
   maximum temperature blank. From then on you'll be
   recording the temperatures from the previous day.
7. Use the weather-forecasting signs on pages 110-111 to
   make predictions.

Lightning

Lightning claims more victims each year than any other natural disaster. Yes, more than floods, earthquakes, tornadoes, hurricanes, tsunamis, and volcanic eruptions. Between 100 and 300 people die each year when lightning strikes, particularly between the months of May and September.

Why? Lightning strikes 100 times a second worldwide. One hundred times every second! And that's with a force of 200 million volts, 300,000 amps, and 8,000 degrees centigrade. Yikes! Even so, you only have one chance in a thousand of being struck—pretty good odds, considering.

Lightning strikes in three ways: within a cloud, cloud-to-cloud, and cloud-to-ground.

Cloud-to-ground lightning can injure you in four different ways:

direct strike, when the bolt hits you directly

splash or side flash, when lightning hits another object but flashes through the air to hit you as well

ground current (the most common way people are injured by lightning), when the lightning strikes a tree, for example, and the current runs to you through the ground or water

the blast effect, when you're thrown by the sudden expansion of air caused by the strike

If you're the victim of a lightning strike you can always hope to be saved by the *flashover effect*. This occurs when the ground-current charge passes over and around you without entering your body.

Lightning causes all kinds of injuries: traumatic, respiratory, neurologic, and cardiac, not to mention burns and everything from loss of hearing to vomiting. Here's yet another situation where knowing CPR could come in handy! Most importantly, never assume a strike victim is fine. Always seek medical attention.

Lightning can strike from a mile away. When you're outdoors without immediate cover, such as a building or a car, start counting when you see that first flash. Count, *"One* one thousand, *two* one thousand," and so on. If you hear the thunder by five, you're within striking range. Because storms move quickly, you need to find a safe spot immediately. If you're lucky the storm will move away from you, but don't count on it and most definitely don't try to outrun it.

There are more don'ts than dos when it comes to finding a safe spot in a thunder storm. Avoid:

bodies of water
low places that can collect water
high places
open places
tall objects
metal objects
wet caves
ditches

Then what *can* you do? Find a small stand of trees and sit with your knees pulled up to your chest, making yourself as small as possible. If you have a sleeping pad with no metal in it, sit on that. If you're in a group, spread out but make sure that every person can be seen by at least one other person in case someone is struck.

If you are trapped above the treeline in an electrical storm, stay away from the seeming protection of depressions and caves: Ground lightning—current from the bolt running through the ground after the strike—is likely to travel right through them. Sitting on a rock surrounded by other high points is your best bet.

Wind Chill

For bragging rights, nothing beats the wind chill chart. On a 30-degree day, with a clear sky and a strong wind, you can claim you camped out when it was 5 degrees outside. Of course, that's because you really will feel that cold. In the primitive, pre–wind chill days you'd have said, "It was 30 degrees out, but it felt a lot colder." Now you can tell just how cold you were.

You can better combat the cold if you're aware of the wind's effect on temperature. A rain jacket and rain pants will cut down on the wind's added power to cool you when you're wet. Most of your body heat radiates out of your head and feet, so keep a knit cap on your head and warm socks and boots on your feet to protect yourself from the wind's chilling effect on even moderate temperatures.

This chart assumes that you are dry. If your body is wet, the wind will have an even stronger cooling effect.

How Fast is the Wind?

These approximate wind speeds can help you gauge wind chill.

Leaves and grass rustle	5 mph
Leaves and small branches sway	10 mph
Branches sway, dead leaves move	15 mph
Small trees sway	20 mph
Whole trees sway	30 mph

Wind Chill Chart

	Actual temperature in degrees Fahrenheit						
Wind (MPH)	40	30	20	10	0	-10	-20
	Wind chill equivalent temperatures						
Calm	40	30	20	10	0	-10	-20
5	35	25	15	5	-5	-15	-25
10	30	15	5	-10	-20	-35	-45
15	25	10	-5	-20	-30	-45	-60
20	20	5	-10	-25	-35	-50	-65
25	15	0	-15	-30	-45	-60	-75
30	10	0	-20	-30	-50	-65	-80
35	10	-5	-20	-35	-55	-70	-85

The Night Sky

The sky at night is made up of thousands of twinkling stars and a few unblinking planets. In ancient times, groupings of stars were transformed by human imagination into pictures called *constellations* (from the Latin *con*, together, and *stella*, star).

Stars can still be used to navigate as they were in ancient times. While the Earth seems to stay still, stars rotate around us daily on an imaginary pole that runs from geographic north to geographic south. *Polaris*, also known as the North Star, is the best star to navigate by because it's located almost directly over the North Pole. You can also use it to find the constellations.

The *Big Dipper* is probably the most famous and easily identified constellation. Its dipper

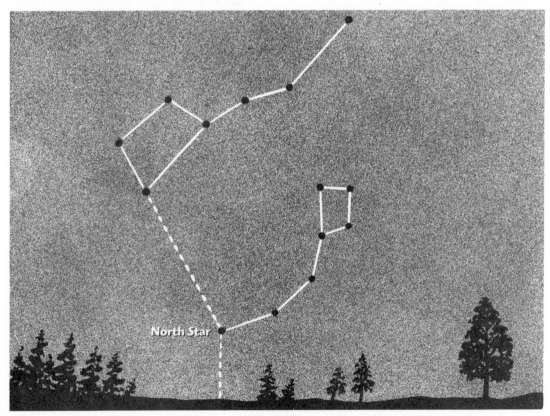

North Star

Using the Big Dipper and Little Dipper to locate the North Star.

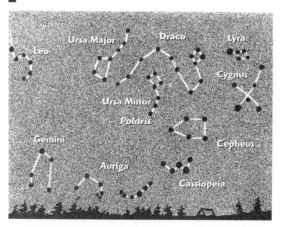

summer sky looking north

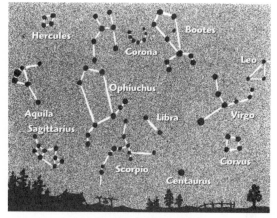

summer sky looking south

(the two stars farthest from the handle) points to Polaris. Four stars form the bowl of the dipper and four form the handle. Looks like three to you? Believe it or not, the second star in the handle is really two stars close together. Polaris is the tip of the handle of the *Little Dipper*.

You can use Polaris and your own hand to determine your approximate latitude. Stretch your arm out in front of you. From your palm just below your little finger to the tip of your up-stretched thumb is about 15 degrees. Measure the distance between the horizon and Polaris against your hand. To refine the measurement, rotate your hand 90 degrees. The vertical distance (represented by the width of your thumb) is 2 to 3 degrees. With your thumb pointing down, the distance from knuckle to knuckle is about 3 degrees. Every degree equals about 60

miles. If Polaris is about 4½ "hands" above the horizon, you're at 45 degrees latitude (roughly equal to Toronto, Canada).

Another way to use stars for direction is to choose a star away from the poles and see which way it travels. Sight its position relative to a tree top, a mountain peak, or even an up-right stick you've placed in the ground. Wait 20 minutes and see where the star has moved. Down? It's moved west. Up? It's moved east. To the right? south. To the left? north.

There are many prominent stars in the sky that form numerous constellations. The following drawings illustrate the summer sky over North America looking both north and south, and the winter sky looking both north and south.

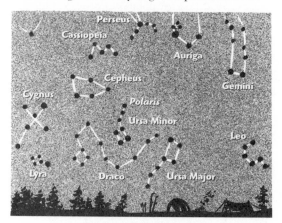

winter sky looking north

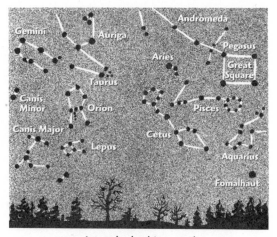

winter sky looking south

Evening Star-Morning Star

ike Geppetto, Pinnochio's toymaker father, many people wish upon the first star they see at night. Geppetto was lucky he got his wish at all, because that evening "star" is often either Venus or Mars, which you can see near the horizon immediately after sunset. At other times of the year these planets are the last objects to fade from the night sky at sunrise, giving them the name "morning star" as well. It wasn't until Roman times that close observation revealed the evening and morning stars to be the same heavenly bodies.

Venus is the closest planet to Earth and, after our own moon, the brightest object in the night sky. When it's the morning star, Venus is so bright it doesn't ever fade from view, and can be tracked throughout the day.

To ancient astronomers planets earned the name *planetes*, meaning wanderers, because they were believed to be stars that traveled across the night sky. This transit across the sky explains why the evening star or morning star is not always the same object. As a planet's orbit takes it around the backside of the sun in relation to Earth, it isn't visible in the night sky.

So what planet are you looking at? That depends on where and when you are observing, but this guide may help you discern the planets visible to the naked eye:

It's a planet if it is very bright and appears to be a constant rather than a twinkling light.

If it is extremely bright, it is Venus, which—when visible—you can see in the east before sunrise and in the west after sunset.

If it is reddish, it is Mars.

If it is not reddish, it is either Jupiter or Saturn. If both are visible, Jupiter is the brighter of the two planets. With good binoculars, or a small telescope, you can see Jupiter's moons or Saturn's rings.

Phases of the Moon

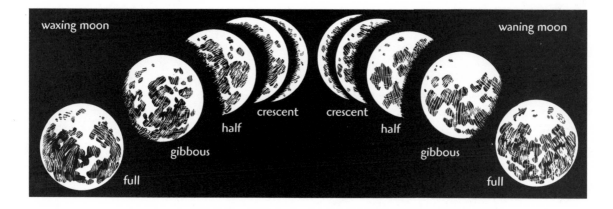

waxing moon · waning moon · crescent · half · gibbous · full · crescent · half · gibbous · full

The phases of the moon are caused by its movement around the Earth and its position in relation to the sun. There are many phases, from the new moon, in which no light or only a fingernail of light is reflected off the surface, to the full moon, in which the moon reflects its full face to the Earth. The moon's phases are also measured in quarters, from the first quarter after the new moon to three-quarters as it nears the full moon and again as it recedes toward a new moon.

Waxing moon: illuminated from the right and growing toward a full moon

Waning moon: illuminated from the left and receding toward a new moon

Gibbous moon: more than half full but less than full

Half moon: half full

Crescent moon: only a crescent illuminated

Apogee moon: at its farthest point, monthly, from the Earth

Perigee moon: at its closest point, monthly, to the Earth

Old Moon or Moon after Yule: first full moon of the new year

Hunter, Snow, or Wolf Moon: February full moon

Crow, Lenten, or Sap Moon: March

Egg or Grass Moon: April

Milk or Planting Moon: May

Rose, Flower, or Strawberry Moon: June

Thunder or Hay Moon: July

Green Corn or Grain Moon: August

Harvest Moon: September

Hunter's Moon: October

Beaver or Frosty Moon: November

Moon before Yule or Long Night Moon: the full moon of December and nearest to the winter solstice

Mammal Signs

A walk though the school cafeteria might make this hard to believe, but mammals are quiet, often solitary, animals. Humans aside, mammals are most often seen in the early morning and at dusk. Finding mammal signs makes it easier to find the animals themselves. Avoid wearing deodorant, perfume, or scented lotions when you go looking for wildlife, since these scents might spook the animals. Keep quiet and move as little as possible when watching for shy mammals.

Pond Signs

Beaver dams and lodges are easy to spot. Trees near the water's edge may also show the telltale marks of a beaver's teeth, even if no

beaver lodge or dam is in sight. Look for swimming beavers just after sunrise and just before sunset. You'll spot a distinctive V shape trailing behind them. You might also hear a tail slap as they swim.

Muddy river banks are a favorite of river otters, whose webbed hind footprints are often indistinct in the smeared mud. Watch the slides in the morning and late afternoon to find the otters at play.

Tree Signs

Several animals leave their marks in tree bark. The habitat and the marks themselves will help you decide what mammal marked the tree. Moose, elk, and deer all eat twigs, and in the spring, they use trees to scrape off the velvet from their antlers. Bears scratch trees and elk also leave tooth marks on aspens that can be hard to distinguish from bear scratches. The elk marks are often at the edge of a grove of trees bordered by a mountain meadow.

Higher up the tree, porcupines leave scars on tree branches as a reminder of their meals. Leave your leather hiking boots outside your tent for another porcupine sign. The porcupines will gnaw right through the boots for the salt your sweaty feet leave in the leather. Porcupines are nocturnal and are seen as a dark blob in a tree by day in an area with porcupine signs.

Predator-Prey Signs

Rodents are often seen in the backcountry, and they are a sure sign that predators are in the area. In mountains where the small, short-tailed vole abounds, you're sure to find weasels. A sizable snowshoe hare population is a good indicator that a Canada lynx is nearby, and mice in a meadow won't be there long without foxes and bobcats moving into the area. If prairie dogs are in a meadow, coyotes will be close by as well.

Of course, mammals aren't the only predators setting their sights on the rodents. You'll also see hawks, owls, and other carnivores if you watch carefully.

Scat

Many animals leave behind distinctive scat (also known as *manure* or *droppings*) as a sign of their presence. Dark, slightly elongated moose "marbles" are often found in the trail. They're about an inch long, much larger than the approximately half-inch-wide pellets left by deer.

Bobcat scat is sometimes found on rocks along trails. A pile of their scat contains the fur and bones of their prey. Fox and coyotes leave two-inch-long straight scat filled with fur and bones. Wolf scat is bigger, often four or more inches long. The scat of dogs and other domestic animals will rarely have the fur and bones that distinguish the scat of wild carnivores.

The pronghorn antelope is the fastest North American land mammal. On short runs it can reach 60 miles per hour, and it can sustain a speed of 30 miles per hour for long distances.

The tiny pigmy shrew is so small and has such a high metabolism (its heart beats 1,200 times a minute) that it must eat several times its own body weight a day to survive. Because it must hunt constantly, it never sleeps.

Alaska's July salmon runs can attract as many as 80 grizzlies in a 100-yard stretch of shallows.

Animal Tracks

lthough most animals try to keep them-selves out of sight of the human eye, many still leave behind evidence of their visit to an area, such as scat (droppings) and tracks.

The best places to look for tracks (since scatological science is a difficult study) is along the edges of water sources where animals come to drink. Other possibilities are in the desert and in snow. If you have access to a farm, prac-tice "tracking" by distinguishing the prints of farm animals. Have a pet? Take it for a walk and see what kind of tracks it makes in mud or snow.

Dogs and Cats

1. The dog family leaves claw marks with its prints; members of the cat family have re-tracted claws that don't show in their paw prints.

2. Cats place their hindfeet in the tracks of their forefeet. Dogs only occasionally place a hindfoot in a forefoot track; usually the hindfoot track is to one side.

3. When a domestic dog runs, its tracks are clearly separate, unlike other members of the dog family—foxes, coyotes, and wolves—who place their hindfeet in the tracks of their forefeet and leave an irregu-lar pattern of three when they run.

Rabbits, Squirrels and Chipmunks

1. Rabbits leave large prints with their hindfeet and smaller prints with their forefeet. Their hopping leaves a track with the hindfeet in front and the forefeet just behind.

2. When a rabbit hops at a normal pace its tracks may be 1 to 2 feet apart, but when it bounds its tracks are 6 to 7 feet apart with one forefoot right behind the other.

3. Squirrels and chipmunks also leave tracks with the hindfeet ahead of the forefeet, but the tracks don't change much, except in distance apart, when they run.

cat

dog

squirrel

rabbit

fox

Otter, Mink, Weasels and Martens

1. The web-footed otter leaves a light impression of the web between the toes of its track.
2. The tracks weave back and forth as otters walk. The paired prints of hindfeet and forefeet are close together when they run.
3. The mink, weasel, and marten have smaller tracks than the otter and leave a walking track similar to the otter's running track. When they run, their tracks often overprint each other and look like three prints rather than four.

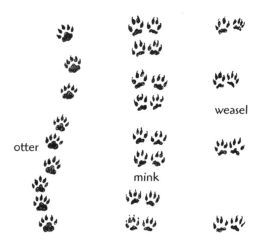

otter

weasel

mink

Raccoons, Skunks, and Porcupines

1. A raccoon print is distinctive because it looks like a thumb and four fingers. The tracks overprint each other when a raccoon walks but separate into the rabbit-like leapfrog pattern when it runs.
2. Skunks leave a very deliberate and distinct pattern when they walk. Their running pattern is peculiar because the left hindfoot leaves a print ahead of the forefeet.
3. Porcupines walk pigeon-toed but leave behind distinct pairs of prints when they run.

raccoon

porcupine

skunk

Deer, Elk, Moose, and Other Hoofed Animals

1. The distinct two-toed hoof print of these mammals is easy to spot in snow and mud.

elk

moose

deer

Make a plaster cast of an animal track

Your best bet for a good cast of an animal track is one made in mud. It would be difficult to carry the necessary supplies on anything but a short hike; you can try making a cast of your pet's track.

You will need:
  plaster of Paris (available at art or hobby shops)
  water
  a strip of cardboard 1½ inches wide x 1 foot long
  an empty tin can
  a small paint brush
  a sponge
  a stick
  a paper clip

1. Brush away all large debris (twigs, stones, etc.) from around the track. If there is any water in the track, sponge it up.

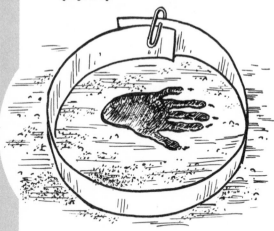

2. Circle the track with the strip of cardboard and fasten the cardboard with the paper clip. Push the cardboard into the mud to about half its width.

3. Put a cup of water in the can and pour the dry plaster slowly into the water, stirring with the stick, until the mixture is as thick and smooth as pancake batter.

4. Pour the plaster slowly over the track (inside the cardboard form) from one side to the other so that any air bubbles can escape before drying into the cast.

5. Allow the plaster to dry for 15 minutes. At that point you can pick it up and scratch any information you'd like to record into the still-damp plaster. You may want to include your initials, the date, the kind of animal, and its name (if it's a pet).

6. Let the cast dry for two days before you remove the cardboard and scrape away the mud.

Snakes

Ever since Eve was tempted by the evil serpent in the Garden of Eden, humans have feared snakes. And why not? With their long fangs, glassy eyes, and scaly skin, they aren't exactly huggable. On the other hand, a snake would rather slither away from you than toward you, and in most cases it will only strike when threatened. As long as you make some noise while you walk (talking with fellow hikers, footsteps sounding clearly), snakes will probably hear you and disappear before you see them.

If you do happen to run into a snake, give it a wide berth if possible. If you can't comfortably step around it, back away and wait for it to leave, as it no doubt will try to do. If it lingers in your path, try scaring it away with loud noises—clapping your hands, blowing a whistle, or shouting. Make extra noise when you pass through brush, deep grass, or piles of dead leaves that may hinder your view of the ground. A number of poisonous snakes dwell near rocky outcroppings and among the boulders in dry streambeds.

You'll generally find coral snakes in the South and Southwest, water moccasins in the wetlands of the South, copperheads throughout the East, and rattlesnakes from coast to coast. However, poisonous snakes hate the cold and aren't found in the Far North where temperatures remain cool to frigid most of the year. If you're in doubt, avoid all snakes but remember that more people die from insect bites each year than from snakebites.

Rattlesnakes

These heavy-bodied snakes usually range from 3 to 5 feet long, although the larger snakes are becoming more rare. Rattlesnakes are distinguished by large blotches and crossbands on either a yellowish or a nearly black background. There are times when the dark color can almost hide the rattlesnake's blotchy pattern.

The most obvious part of a rattlesnake is the rattle at the end of its tail. This is often used as a warning to predators, but don't count on hearing it because the snake may also choose to lie still.

Another distinctive feature of the rattlesnake, shared by the copperhead and the water moccasin, is its infamous diamond-shaped head.

Copperheads

Copperheads are 2 to 3 feet in length and fairly thick. They feature brown or chestnut hourglass-shaped crossbands on a lighter background ranging from reddish-brown to chestnut to gray-brown. The crossbands are outlined in a darker color so the snake is perfectly camouflaged among dead leaves. Other, nonpoisonous, snakes imitate this pattern but not so distinctly as the copperhead, and they lack the diamond-shaped head.

Coral or Harlequin Snake

These little snakes rarely exceed 3 feet in length and their markings are imitated by plenty of other snakes. Just remember the saying "Red on yellow will kill a fellow," and you won't confuse it with snakes that lack the coral's particular pattern of red, yellow, and black bands. The broader bands of red and blue-black are separated by narrow bands of yellow. This is the most venomous of all the poisonous snakes in the United States. An *antivenin* must be used to counteract the poison of this snake.

copperhead

coral snake

water moccasin

Water Moccasin or Cottonmouth

These large snakes are dull olive to brownish in color but paler on the sides, which have indistinct wide, dark bands. Up to 5 feet in length, water moccasins are very stout and have an abruptly tapering tail as well as eye shields. Next to the cobra, they're one of the meanest-looking snakes around, and the meanest poisonous snake in the United States.

Treating Poisonous Snakebites

If you're bitten by a poisonous snake your reaction will be immediate. The area around the bite will discolor and swell, your pulse will quicken, and you'll feel weak. You may also feel nauseated, vomit, and experience fading vision and shock within an hour.

Don't apply a tourniquet unless it's absolutely necessary, because this can cause more damage than the snakebite. Nor should you cut and suck the wound. Instead, reduce the amount of circulation in the bite area by keeping the victim still, applying a cold and wet cloth to the area, or using a constricting band. Seek immediate medical attention.

If you're venturing far from medical attention you'll need to carry a snakebite kit to provide emergency care on your own.

Ticks and Disease

Ticks carry two very serious diseases: Lyme disease and Rocky Mountain spotted fever. These illnesses are hard for doctors to diagnose because they both resemble many other diseases. Once diagnosed, however, each of these diseases is easily treated with antibiotics. They're also easy to avoid if you take some precautions. When you're walking through woods and brush, wear light-colored clothes and check yourself frequently for ticks.

To remove a tick already embedded in your skin, use a pair of tweezers to grab its body and as much of the head as possible. Pull the tick straight out. Never twist a tick as you remove it.

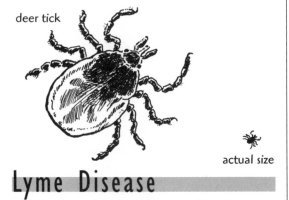

deer tick

actual size

Lyme Disease

Lyme disease causes fever, headache, and pain and stiffness in joints and muscles. Left untreated, Lyme disease causes serious complications, including brain injury and crippling arthritis. The disease first appears with flulike symptoms (fatigue, headache, muscle and joint pain, swollen glands) and a skin rash with a bright red border. It can also lead to serious heart complications and attack the liver, eyes, kidney, spleen, and lungs. If you suspect you have Lyme disease, see a doctor immediately.

Rocky Mountain Spotted Fever

This tick-borne disease is misnamed today, since it's as common on the eastern seaboard as it is in the Rocky Mountains. (North Carolina routinely has the highest number of cases reported.) Ticks transmit the disease four to six hours after attaching themselves to you, so your best defense is to check yourself often for ticks.

Headache and fever are the most common symptoms. Other symptoms include a rash on wrists, hands, ankles, or feet; loss of appetite; and abdominal or chest pain. The rash can be a late sign and may not appear until the disease has progressed far enough to make it difficult to treat. Bleeding problems, including coagulation abnormalities, will result if the disease goes untreated. About 5 percent of victims die from the disease.

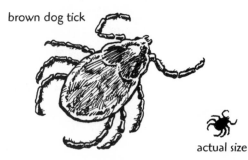

brown dog tick

actual size

Coniferous Trees

There are more than 600 trees native to the United States alone, and these are divided into two large groups: conifers, or cone-bearers, and broad-leaf, or deciduous, trees.

Conifers are also known as evergreens because they don't lose their needles (scalelike leaves) when the weather turns cold. There are five main types of conifers:

1. Pines. These are easy to recognize by their straight trunks, which are free of branches partway up. To determine what type of pine it is, look closely at the needles. How many needles are there to a cluster—five, three, or two?

2. Spruces and firs. These are often used as Christmas trees. Spruce needles are four-sided and grow singly all around the branch; fir needles are flat and appear to be arranged in two rows on the sides of the branch.

3. Hemlocks. These large trees have small cones and small, flat, round-tipped leaves.

4. Cedars, junipers, and cypresses. The leaves of cedars are tiny, bright green scales arranged like shingles on flattened twigs. Junipers have two kinds of leaves, scaly and flat or awl-like and prickly. Their cones are berrylike and blue. Cypresses grow only in swamplands and are distinguished by their "knees," or cone-shaped stumps. The bald cypress loses it needles every winter.

5. Sequoias. These are the largest conifers and include the giant redwoods, which can grow as high as 350 feet and reach a diameter of 25 feet. Found only in California, they are also the oldest trees in world—many are over 4,000 years old.

Deciduous Trees

These broad-leaf trees get their name from the Latin word *decidere*, or to fall off, because they lose their leaves each year. There are dozens of families of trees in the deciduous group, including:

1. Willows and poplars. Includes aspens and cottonwoods.

2. Nut trees. Includes walnuts, hickories, pecans, and butternuts.

3. Birches. Includes hornbeams, alders, and the birch (whose bark was once used to build canoes).

4. Beeches and chestnuts. The beech is known for its smooth, pale gray bark.

5. Oaks. Includes white oaks, black oaks, and live oaks.

6. Elm and hackberry trees. The latter looks like an elm but grows berrylike fruit.

7. Magnolia and tulip trees. The yellow-green flower of the tulip tree makes it distinctive.

8. Custard and tea trees. Includes pawpaws and sassafras.

9. Gums and sycamores. The gum is known for its spiny fruit and the sycamore for its patchwork bark.

10. Plum and cherry trees. There are dozens of varieties of these wild fruit trees.

11. Maples. Known for their winged fruit and brilliant autumn foliage.

12. Buckeyes. Named for their large, shiny, brown fruit which looks like the eye of a deer.

13. Ashes. Feathery crowns of dark green leaves make the ash distinctive.

Make a leaf print

You can also print ferns, grasses, feathers, and anything else with a distinctive pattern. You will need:

a leaf to print	a roller to spread the ink
a pane of glass	a spoon
newspaper	rags or paper towels
paper to print on	turpentine or paint remover
oil-based ink	

1. Cover your work area with newspaper. Place the leaf on newspaper, vein side up.

2. Ink your roller by squeezing a small amount of ink onto the pane of glass and pushing the roller over the glass until it's covered with ink.

3. Push the roller over the leaf two or three times.
4. Slip a clean sheet of newspaper under the inked leaf.

5. Place the sheet of paper for your leaf impression over the leaf. Don't move the piece of paper after placing it. Fold a piece of newspaper and lay it over the print paper.

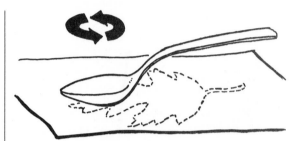

6. With one hand, hold the papers so they don't slip. Use the other hand to rub the back of the spoon over all of the newspaper. Rub up and down and back and forth.

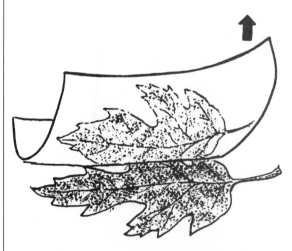

7. Remove the newspaper, then carefully lift the print paper.
8. The leaf print is complete. You can either continue to print or clean up. Make sure you clean the roller, your hands, and the pane of glass before the ink dries. The turpentine will help remove the ink. Be sure to wash your hands thoroughly after using the paint remover.

Poisonous Plants

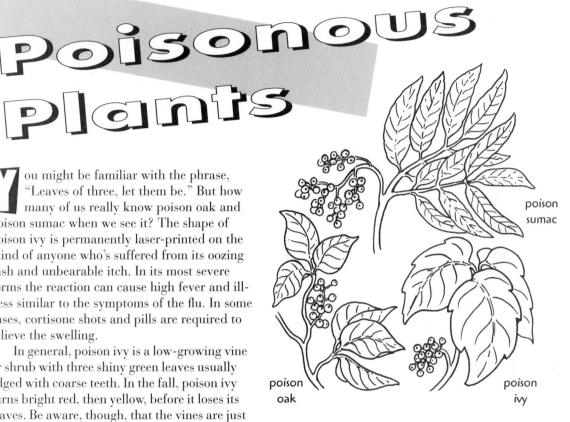

poison sumac

poison oak

poison ivy

You might be familiar with the phrase, "Leaves of three, let them be." But how many of us really know poison oak and poison sumac when we see it? The shape of poison ivy is permanently laser-printed on the mind of anyone who's suffered from its oozing rash and unbearable itch. In its most severe forms the reaction can cause high fever and illness similar to the symptoms of the flu. In some cases, cortisone shots and pills are required to relieve the swelling.

In general, poison ivy is a low-growing vine or shrub with three shiny green leaves usually edged with coarse teeth. In the fall, poison ivy turns bright red, then yellow, before it loses its leaves. Be aware, though, that the vines are just as poisonous as the leaves. Poison ivy grows everywhere in the continental United States except for California and parts of adjacent states. It's particularly common in the south and goes by a number of names, including poison oak, three-leaf ivy, poison creeper, climbing sumac, markweed, picry, and mercury.

Poison oak, a close relation of poison ivy, is also known by the infamous three leaflets. The leaflets can have from three to seven lobes each and the leaves are hairy underneath. Poison oak (also known as Western poison oak) grows only in California and parts of adjacent states where (to add to the confusion) it's also known as poison ivy or yeara.

The third plant in the dastardly trio is poison sumac. It flourishes in damp places as a shrub or a small tree from 5 to 25 feet tall. Also related to poison ivy, it has compound leaflets, which are smooth and grow in a V-shape from the midrib of the stem. It has drooping white berries. Known by several names—swamp sumac, poison elder, poison ash, poison dogwood, and thunderwood—it grows in most of the eastern third of the United States.

If you realize you've had a brush with one of the "poisons," take a cool or cold bath as soon as possible, using soap to clean yourself completely. Afterwards, use calamine lotion, Benadryl cream, or any poison ivy-specific medication to help relieve whatever itching and inflammation there might be. Cortisone creams also help. If your reaction is severe, see a doctor. About 50 percent of the population is susceptible to extreme reactions from poison plants; of those 50 percent, reactions vary from person to person and can even change in an individual.

The Outdoor Skills Quiz

Test your knowledge of leave-no-trace camping and hiking as well as your outdoor skills. Some answers are worth one point and others are worth two points. If you get no points, do us all a favor and stay out of the backcountry! For 1 to 10 points, you're a certified couch potato—read this book and try again. For 11 to 15 points, you're ready for the outdoors. For more than 16 points, you're a backcountry guide. Hint: The answers are practical and not always at the extreme of leave-no-trace. Answers are on page 136.

1. You're walking a trail with two other hikers. Three miles in from the road, one of the other hikers slips off a steep slope. The hiker is now 20 feet down a steep embankment with what seems to be a badly broken leg and a vicious bruise on the forehead. You should:

a. cut through the woods to the nearest road and flag down a car for help.

b. splint the leg and help the hiker walk back to the trailhead.

c. stay with the injured hiker while the third member of your group hikes back to the trailhead for help.

d. act like you've never seen the injured hiker before, finish your hike, and watch the evening news to find out what happened.

2. You're camping at a primitive campsite equipped with a privy that has more flies and smells worse than the south end of a northbound moose. What do you do when nature calls?

a. head to the woods with a trowel, keeping at least 200 feet from any water source and well away from camp to spread out the impact on the campsite and your nose.

b. use the privy.

c. pack out all wastes in a plastic bag.

d. wait until you get home two days later.

3. You reach your goal for the day's hike, an established primitive campsite along the trail. The two campfire rings are full of half-burned trash. What do you do?

a. build a fire in each ring to finish burning the trash.

b. take both rings apart, scatter the rocks in the woods, and pack out the trash.

c. dismantle one fire ring, scatter the rocks away from the campsite, and pack out the trash from both rings.

d. build a fire in one ring and leave the other one in case more campers arrive later.

4. Bushwhacking straight up or down a mountain and bypassing the switchbacks is:

a. a mortal sin punishable by a lifetime in hell under any circumstances.

b. allowable for beating a quick retreat off a treeless summit to get away from an electrical storm booming overhead.

c. a good idea if you're tired.

d. OK if nobody else is around to follow your bad example.

5. Banana peels, peanut shells, and other "natural trash" should be:

a. eaten. You have to take the bad parts with the good when trying to leave no trace.

b. buried out of sight of camp.

c. scattered in the woods to rot.

d. packed out with the rest of your trash.

6. Tents, rain jackets, and pack covers are sold in a variety of colors. You should buy them in:

a. earth tones to blend in with the surroundings.

b. international orange so hunters won't confuse you for deer and other big-game animals.

c. bright colors to signal airplanes in case you get lost.

d. white for summer gear to reflect heat and keep you cooler, and black for winter gear to absorb heat and keep you warm.

7. If you're dumped overboard on a whitewater rafting or canoe trip, you should:

a. swim across the rapids in the crawl stroke to get to the bank as fast as you can.

b. pull someone else overboard to help you in the rapids.

c. pinch yourself to make sure it isn't all a bad dream.

d. point your feet downstream and float through the rapids, getting out at the closest calm spot.

8. When you're collecting wood for a campfire, be sure to:

a. get enough wood to keep the fire burning all night in case you get a really good joke-telling session going.

b. cut down trees that look like they're dead anyway.

c. collect wood out of sight of the camp, picking up only dead and downed wood.

d. not get any, because you shouldn't build fires.

9. You've been hiking all afternoon in a steady drizzling rain. It's 45 degrees out and your backpacking partner has been shivering and complaining about being cold. Now he's slurring his words and talking about going to sleep early without dinner. You should:

a. set up the tent and keep quiet while he drifts off to sleep.

b. get him out of his wet clothes, fire up the stove, and get him something hot to drink and a good warm meal.

c. hike the 8 miles back to the car together. Your partner has hypothermia and needs medical attention.

d. strip off all your clothes and climb into a sleeping bag with your partner to warm him up.

10. After you clean the dishes in camp, you should get rid of the water you washed them in by:

a. packing it out.

b. pouring it into a swift-moving creek where it will be cleaned as it rushes through the rocks.

c. packing out any leftover food scraps and scattering the little bit of water well away from camp and at least 200 feet from a water source.

d. swallowing the leftover water, if you didn't use soap. It's only leftover food anyway.

Answers:

1. c. Don't move a badly injured person unless you have extensive first aid training and are properly equipped to do so. Give yourself 2 points for c and no points for any other answer.

2. b. Give yourself 2 points for using a smelly privy. You get 1 point for answer a. You should have used the privy, but at least you followed leave-no-trace guidelines when you hit the woods.

3. c. At an established site it's overly optimistic to assume that other campers will forego a fire. But taking the second ring apart will confine the later use to one site. Give yourself 2 points for answer c and one point for answer b, which takes leave-no-trace practices a bit too far for an established campsite.

4. b. Let's be realistic. Safety should come first, but bend the rules only if you're really in danger. Give yourself 2 points for answer b and just one point for taking things too far with answer a.

5. d. Pack out all trash, natural or otherwise. It takes banana peels and peanut shells too long to rot in the woods and they could be dug up by animals if buried. Give yourself 2 points for answer d and no points for any other answer. (Eat peels and shells if you like, but you won't get any points for it here.)

6. a. Give yourself 2 points for selecting gear that won't clash with the outdoors. It will make your camp less intrusive on your fellow campers' wilderness experience. Give yourself 1 point for answer b, though, because an international or-

ange coat, vest, or pack cover will make winter hiking safer in areas frequented by hunters. You don't get 2 points because getting all your gear in orange is a little too much to expect.

7. d. Keep your feet pointed downstream to absorb the shock of running into rocks. Give yourself 2 points for d and no points for other answers. Trying to swim across the current in big rapids will only send you over a falls sideways and unprotected. Work with the current, not against it.

8. c or d. Give yourself 2 points for either response. It's true that you should forego a campfire whenever possible, but the question did ask what to do if you're going to have a fire. Gathering wood away from the campsite will prevent that surface-of-the-moon, picked-over look that well-worn campsites get.

9. b. You get 2 points for recognizing signs of hypothermia, even when the temperature is well above freezing. You should have to take away a point (but don't) if you laughed at answer d. If your hiking buddy doesn't have dry clothes and you can't get enough warm food and drink into him to stop the shivering, the next step is to use your own body heat to warm him up. Don't worry about how this story will sound when you tell it at school—your buddy's life is at stake.

10. c. You get 2 points for this answer. Go ahead and give yourself 1 point each for either a or d. They're a little extreme to be practical, but either of these would work.

Index